Psychotherapy
and the
Poverty Patient

Psychotherapy and the Poverty Patient

E. Mark Stern, Editor
Iona College, New Rochelle, New York

The Psychotherapy Patient Series
E. Mark Stern, Editor

The Haworth Press
New York • London

Psychotherapy and the Poverty Patient has also been published as *The Psychotherapy Patient*, Volume 7, Numbers 1/2 1990.

The Haworth Press, Inc., 10 Alice Street, Binghamton, NY 13904-1580
EUROSPAN/Haworth, 3 Henrietta Street, London WC2E 8LU England

Library of Congress Cataloging-in-Publication Data

Psychotherapy and the poverty patient / E. Mark Stern, Editor
    p. cm.
    Has also been published as the Psychotherapy patient : v. 7, no. 1/2, 1990.
    Includes bibliographical references.
    ISBN 1-56024-066-0
    1. Poor—Mental health. 2. Psychotherapy. 3. Poverty—Psychological aspects. I. Stern, E. Mark. 1929- .
    [DNLM: 1. Medical Indigency—psychology. 2. Physician—Patient Relations. 3. Poverty—psychology. 4. Psychotherapy. W1 PS87 v. 7 no. 1/2 / WM 420 P97535535]
RC451.4.P6P78   1990
616.89'14—dc20
DNLM/DLC   90-5191
for Library of Congress   CIP

Psychotherapy and the Poverty Patient

CONTENTS

ABOUT THE EDITOR

E. Mark Stern, EdD, is Professor in the Graduate Division of Pastoral and Family Counseling, Graduate School of Arts and Sciences, Iona College, New Rochelle, New York. A Diplomate in Clinical Psychology of the American Board of Professional Psychology and a Fellow of the American Psychological Association and the American Psychological Society, Dr. Stern is President of the Division of Humanistic Psychology, APA. He is in private practice of psychotherapy with offices in New York City and Dutchess County, New York. Dr. Stern completed his clinical studies at Columbia University (1955) and at the Institute of the National Psychological Association for Psychoanalysis.

Psychotherapy
and the
Poverty Patient

The Poverty Patient:
A Preface

There is an old saying that poverty is the wicked soul's tempter, the good soul's desolation, and the melancholy soul's noose. The ancient Greeks considered poverty to be the mother of self-control, while today's world sees the quest for material needs as the totality of personal enterprise.

To be certain, hunger and homelessness are the perniciousness of an otherwise fed and housed humankind. Yet there are other forms of poverty, not always related to indigence or destitution. Whether defined as authentic or culturally determined, this other poverty enters the psychological realm. It is the personal paradox which can easily mistake the realities of existence for the demands of material satisfaction and greed. This poverty is made all the more poorer still by a society constantly flooded by advertised wants and riddled by a creeping neglect of the intrinsic value of the individual.

In view of the awesomeness of personal poverty, the psychotherapist, much like his or her practitioner counterparts in religion and philosophy, becomes the appropriate conciliator or honest broker between unrevealed necessity and inner neglect.

Psychotherapy and the Poverty Patient is one other bridge across the many facets of working with the psychologically and materially impoverished. It is far from a united attempt. Rather like other publications in this series, this monograph takes a wide-angled look at a mottled contemporary issue which presents both clinical and philosophical challenges to the practicing psychotherapist.

E. Mark Stern
Editor

1

"If I Were a Rich Man":
Reflections on a Poverty
of the Spirit

E. Mark Stern

SUMMARY. Poverty is explored both as a value and as an attribute. Probing the question of poverty and the soul, this examination borrows from the fictional Tevye popularized in the musical *A Fiddler on the Roof* and from the French zealot Simone Weil. At length, a psychotherapy patient's rapidly shifting moods are reviewed within the context of his experience of poverty. Beyond financial, vocational, and social constraints, this patient ultimately proved capable of drawing on his poverty as the hub of his engagement with life.

POVERTY AND THE SOUL

Tevye is a fictional village dairy merchant in the Shalom Aleichem based musical, *Fiddler on the Roof*. Though a perennial victim of anti-Semitic oppression and borderline poverty, he finds himself able to sing nostalgically of what it might be like to be a "rich man." Hard as his life may be for him, Tevye nevertheless typifies the nature of a hopeful poverty, enriched even more by the bitter-sweetness of a strong cultural tradition. Were Tevye to have his prayers answered and actually become a "rich man," there would have been the risk of a vacuous existence.

E. Mark Stern, EdD, Columbia University, 1955, Diplomate in Clinical Psychology of the American Board of Professional Psychology, Fellow of the American Psychological Association, is Professor, Graduate Division of Pastoral and Family Counseling, Iona College, New Rochelle, NY, and is in private practice in New York City and Clinton Corners, NY. Mailing address: 215 E. 11 St., New York, NY 10003.

Tevye, a milk vendor by trade, is both comical and tragic since his poverty attests to a vast personal wellspring. Standing on the precipice of persecution and oppression, Tevye and his Eastern European Jewish community remain central to the broken fortunes which embody the many ambiguities of uncertainty. Tevye is thus the richest since it is he who finds contentment with the least.

No legitimate case can ever be made for romanticizing the plight of the neediest. Being desperately poor leaves a frightening residue pool of psychic scarring. Yet even the most pervasive wounds can be signs of potential transformation. Poverty, even at its worst, must be seen a worthy calling.

There is, however, a danger in romanticizing poverty. Yet it would be even more insensitive to neglect the special vantages of being poor. The quality of Tevye's poverty linked him to the hard lessons of survival which in turn had become his touchstone with those in even greater jeopardy. Simone Weil (Coles 1986), a 1930s and '40s French radical social critic, deeply identified with the poor and oppressed, doubted that slum clearances, better schools, or even more political empowerment would necessarily signal a definitive upward movement. To her, the menace of an uncaring materialism is evidence of a downward psychic direction.

Weil was an anarchist whose reverence for the poor was further enhanced by her spiritual searchings. Her personal involvements and identification with the underclassed bore witness to a unique relationship between economic and spiritual poverty. Weil's legacy periscopes the necessity of loosening the grips of personal materialism as primary to authentic existence.

Weil and the fictional Tevye are reminders of the complex dynamics of poverty and its relationship to social sensibility and conscience. As a result of her associations with the extreme Left, Simone Weil had understood the potential for abusive power. Though an active union organizer, she knew that the the unbridled claims of the collective utopian ideas led by the few would in the end only rob the individual of the significance of a drive for individual sanctification. Poverty challenges the soul and is challenged by the Faustian promises of a racing technology. The individual, once rooted in a somewhat intense interplay between good and evil, has been mollified. Personhood, rather than social and economic deprivation, has been paupered by the very technocratic forces which have promised it secular salvation. And while poverty in its many forms embodies neediness, it can also foster the realization that there can be no authentic existence without the paupered soul. The mention of such neediness is not intended to deprecate the tragedy of social injustice and poverty. Rather it is meant to emphasize the universal home-lessness and searchings of the soul. Since there is no defined safety zone, my psychotherapy practice fuses search and surrender.

PSYCHOTHERAPY:
SEARCH AND SURRENDER

Elvin had learned to ride the tides of insecurity. Armed with less than a high school education, he was at 36 years of age living in a bare studio apartment in a run-down section of an outer city suburb. He was referred to me because of what he termed being in and out of "speeded up" behavior. These mood swings were serious enough to place his job as a bus repairman in jeopardy. As it was, he was barely making a living wage because of his unwillingness to put in false overtime claims.

Earlier in the year, Elvin had been advised by the medical exam-iner to take a leave of absence and was placed on medication to lessen his excitability. There were concerns that the pills would make it dangerous to work with heavy equipment. The psychiatrist who referred him to me believed he could better be helped by psy-chological means.

Elvin was concerned that his immediate supervisor, along with several other workers, were out to undermine his ethical standards. According to him, the entire crew had been illegally signing the worksheets for unearned overtime. He was both disdainful of such behavior and fearful that it would contribute to his ultimate down-fall.

The matter went far beyond work. It was not hard to recognize Elvin's rage nor surprising to learn about his periodic outbursts: "This guy would look at me," he said, "and I walked up to him and let him know that I paid for my own drinks."

"Something about his glare seemed to be accusing you of being dishonest?"

"You've got it," he said.

"Do you suppose he was trying to make you dishonest? . . . Like if you were a dishonest sort then he'd be sure you'd stoop to just about anything."

"And where do you think that'd get me?"

"It's hard for me to tell. . . . I guess," I said sometime a little later, "it'd waken all of the things you're most afraid of."

"Hell," he said, "you may think the same thing."

"How so?" I asked.

"You might think of me as a nothing."

"You mean I'd try to take what was rightfully yours?"

"I think that sort of thing a lot," he answered. Then he spoke about how ashamed he was of having such thoughts. He moved in and out of thoughts with great rapidity. "I sure don't want to steal anybody's money," he said.

"And you would think that I thought you would?" After a slight pause: "If you had no food—were starving say, or even without caring, could you then imagine stealing?"

"No sir," he answered.

Elvin was, if not without food, certainly without much love. Other than rare encounters with street prostitutes, there were no women in his life. "I sometimes wonder, Elvin," I said, "that if some really great woman came along and tried to get close to you, you'd give her short shrift. It's like you're so protected by having just nothing and no one." (Later) "And Elvin, if someone looked at you and said, 'This is an honest man,' you'd be looking for a slight smirk on his face—you know, the kind of smirk which would say to you, 'You're a liar, a thief, a man who might just about say anything.'"

"Well who knows, maybe he would think that he was right. I don't steal. But I have. I could tell you, but I don't know what you'd do with it."

"Maybe nothing at all," I said. "But I'd sure be interested in knowing about everything that has ever made you feel like what it's like to be a person."

Elvin wanted his therapy to be something of a confession. And still he wanted not to be discovered. He spoke of feeling ashamed of what he didn't have. He felt that he'd have to protect himself from some of my sort "of knowing." He feared my disapproving of his discontinuation of his medication. Did such discontinuation require that he become less excitable with others? he wondered.

I said that I had no opinion regarding the medicine. I did say that I didn't think the medication had much to do with how ashamed he was feeling. Shame had always defined much of his existence. I told him that I wasn't even interested in taking away his shame. "Nothing I intend to do will leave you any the poorer."

"You know," he said, "I get scared of having nothing."

"You say that you've got plenty of nothing?" I was interested in even the barest traces of his own controls.

"Even my nothing could fit into a small-sized suitcase. But if I ever open it — " He stopped short.

"When you open it?"

He folded his arms, and looked straight ahead at me: "It may be nothing, but it sure as hell has a conscience."

"What has a conscience?" I asked.

"Everything that I have has a conscience."

"And you, Elvin, do you have a conscience?"

"I'd sometimes like to trade it in. But I wasn't trained that way."

"Training is basic."

"I sure would trade it in for a chance to do something else."

"Wouldn't you need it for something else?"

"I'd need it for doing what you do," he said.

"Would you like to do what I do, Elvin?"

"I think so, but I would sure be sure that I kept on time."

"Sure be sure," I repeated. "Sounds like that's what it's all about?"

Elvin didn't reply for some time. He seemed to be wavering about what to say. Finally: "You don't keep to schedule a lot of the times I come."

I felt defensive. It was true I have never been reliable with schedules. And I have been aware that my frequent latenesses could be interpreted as manipulative and unprofessional. Yet I began to see my troubles with time as providing a possible bridge to Elvin. "You're absolutely correct. I'm lousy with being on time."

Elvin made some self-conscious protests of not really minding. I was tempted to leave it at that. No matter how many years of practice, I find time issues managerial dilemmas. Time for me has always had something to do with my view of shortages. I've often felt the poorer with the rapid advancing of time. So I've created an excessively busy schedule which leaves me little time to answer phone calls or to feel rich with leisure. So poorly have I budgeted my time that I often arrive at airports much too early and with no less anxiety that I may be late. I'll not go into my own time loops. Needless to say, I regard the "terror" of time an aspect of my own poverty.

"We are birds of a feather," I said. "We both seem bent on fears that we may be doing the wrong thing. You and I live on the edge — you with money and with other people's time distortions, and me with time and a vague uncomfortable feeling that I hurt others through my mismanagement of time."

The unpredictability of the outcome of self-disclosure in my psychotherapy practice has always filled me with feelings of borderline anarchy. Elvin seemed to either not notice, or regard my confession as promise that the time deal would finally work out and that he would no longer have to glare at the old magazines in my waiting room for a third and fourth time.

I admitted that there was something disquieting about his comments about accusing me of being unreliable. I wasn't all that sure that my promises to the contrary would really take, or that I could now honestly promise that I would be precisely on time ever. "There's more power in where you sit than you realize," I said.

Elvin sensed that my intent was not to put either of us down. "You mean I have something to say?" he smiled. "I'd like to think I could do the kind of work you do, but I don't fool myself. I'm just a poor guy."

"Your poverty is a power that doesn't come at a small price. . . . Maybe there is purpose in where you happen to be."

"Hell," he replied, "I think I'd just about be anywhere else."

"You'd rather be rich man?"

He said that he wouldn't then have to care so much about how others drained him. "No one is satisfied with what they've got. I just wish others wouldn't try to draw me in on their shenanigans."

"Why shouldn't they? Remember," I reminded him, "you owned up to being the guy with plenty of nothing."

"So what are you saying, that I should just sit there and take it?" he asked.

"Take it? Obviously. Other people envy your plenty of nothing."

"Are you mad?" he replied. "Why those guys are breaking company codes and safety rules. They make me so damn angry, but I guess I should be a little held back."

"For what reason?" I asked.

"They are not above revenge. They count on the extra cash in their pockets. Hell, I could find myself splotched out in some doorway or something like that."

"So there are consequences? But don't they even just mask the fact that you are feeling left out, even though you're doing what's right for you?"

Elvin turned away. He said that he'd rather be poor any time. He saw his mode of being as real, personal, and definite. "I don't want to feel taken in by guys who just want a free ride at someone else's expense," he said. "I couldn't live from day to day with the feeling that I could be their stooge. I couldn't live that way and still face my Maker." Yet he was concerned that his "old zip" had started to run dry.

There was helplessness and anger in his opting to be poor and honest. I linked the helplessness and rage to others who elected to remain similarly disenfranchised. He would need to learn to reverence his "choice" even as he began to focus on ways of better managing his discontent. "I'd stand up for my principles even if it means I'm out on the streets."

Elvin decided to put some of his concerns into action. He wrote a letter to the Transportation Authority which he asked me to edit, outlining the prevailing dishonest practices in his job. He felt that he had tried his best to probe a centerless web of fabrications and falsehoods. The reply was polite and dismissing. "You can only do what you're doing for a pretty hefty price tag," I reminded him. "You'll never be a rich man." But he knew that his option for poverty was necessary even as he was beginning to realize that his problems preceded his job. He was, by choice or destiny, an outsider. He was more than willing to pay attention to the consequences of being radically apart. This crisis of otherness, forced

Elvin to be not only in constant touch with his fury, but also with his self-respect and courage.

Elvin grew up in a household riddled with contradictions and conflicts. His father had been imprisoned in his youth. He spent months at a time out of work barely maintaining a fragile foothold on sanity. The family knew that it was better do without than for that the father to return to his "old schemes."

Elvin's mother had effectively withdrawn from her children when they seemed to need her most. She was an overwhelming, suspicious woman waiting for her husband and children to turn on her. "Those years were like walking on rotten eggs. Mom was always accusing someone. I guess," he said. "Mom seemed to think that my father was having affairs with other women."

"And your feeling?" I asked.

"I just couldn't see it. He cowered too much."

"Could it have been," I speculated, "that she both feared and wanted to see him as an effective man? It wouldn't have mattered had he robbed banks or slept with other women."

"What she would keep saying was that we were poor. And she'd point fingers at him. Nothing would help. I felt that I ought to be able to do something to lighten the financial burden. Hey, we were eating potatoes every night for weeks at a time."

"Sounds as if you were on the verge of starvation."

"I've always been on that verge. And you know something, despite what I went through growing up, that was the one part I could care less about."

"You learned how to make do?"

"Yeah, and I wouldn't have known where our food came from if all of a sudden it appeared."

"It would have come from illegalities? Or from other women?"

"That's what it felt like to me. And that's what I kept hearing underneath everything else."

"So did you help out?"

"It may seem crazy, but no job would ever do. I was afraid like I am now. I was just never one of the boys. I couldn't accept tips from old people when I delivered groceries. I'd have to find ways of getting it back to them. I hated pumping gas, because I could never figure out just what was owed by the customer. You had to add on some tax—write down what was owed by people who had accounts at the station—and after a while I just didn't show, and believe me, I had nothing to show for what seemed like hours of different sorts of jobs. Meanwhile I was fighting with everybody."

"At home too?"

"You could hardly speak enough to fight. Then my father got a stroke. He was never going to be able to say another word. We went on welfare. No one in the family seemed able to pull for themselves."

"I'm not quite sure what pulling for yourself means," I said. "But are you giving yourself the right to deserve some credit?"

"You know me, I don't feel as if I have, or have ever had anything."

Although Elvin was not penniless, he did insist on his needy circumstances. He felt himself convoluted, with all lighthouses darkened. His "speeded up" condition served as an analogy for the sullen slowness of his day-to-day existence. Yet, by his own admission, he reminded me that he was "not that bad off." More importantly, he wished to be confirmed on his unique survival qualities. It was here that the potential for collaborating with Elvin bore most fruit.

Elvin felt imperiled by his "added up speed" which did and did not make him feel "good." These very real sensations of speed were for Elvin like being accosted by an untamable carousel. I respected his perils and his tenacity in trying to manage them. Through it all, Elvin's poverty was for him both blight and fearsome challenge. His major strengths seemed determined by the intensity of his remaining poor. And yet the paradox of Elvin's poverty was like Tevye's. He too yielded to the notion of becoming "a rich man." But *because* of being possessed of poverty, he was forced to deal with the core of uncertainty. He could do little other than not allow himself to resign to the ever-present temptations to give in to the dishonest plots which were all too popular with his fellow workers.

Elvin, although aspiring to aspects of "the good life," chose not to circumvent or disengage himself from his bare cupboard. Similar to the stork who, in an attempt to disentangle himself from a mud bank, thought, "I'll push my beak even further into the muck in order to free myself.'' Releasing his legs, he found himself upright on his beak. And despite reversals from beak to legs and from legs to beak, there he remained. Yet each time he reversed positions, the change in positions provided its own change in perspective.

"I find myself back and forth in my moods. Sometimes it feels like I am a rich man. You know it has nothing necessarily to do with what I have. The feeling has happened when I've been laid off for months at a time. I can't explain it, but I guess it's all OK.''

"And the other times?'' I asked.

"You know, I'm glad that's being raised. The other times reek with fear. I want to strike out at anyone and everyone. It's like no one fits in with where I am.''

"How do you account for the shift?''

"I haven't been able to.'' Elvin looked pensive.

"Perhaps,'' I volunteered, "you are not as helpless as you think you are. Maybe you are busily reordering the way the feelings come. When you experience scarcity, it can feel either freeing or burdensome.''

"You say I'm not helpless to feel the way I want to?''

"Not quite in the sense that you can just wish away the down moods. But you can decide to go with them — find out what they want of you.''

"But then I'm really in danger of causing the crash of a bus or hitting someone.''

"Sounds to me,'' I said, "that that danger is all the more real if you try to defy your mood. I didn't suggest that you find out what the mood wants *from* you. It was what it wanted *of* you. The difference being that people fight mostly their way out of situations rather than allowing themselves to be owned by them. Like in judo, you don't react to a punch by returning one of greater force. The idea is to go along with the thrust. You allow it to possess you.''

Elvin understood me. He had known the difference between being and trying to become. Poverty was a state of his existence. It was the present reality for him. Without reverting to the romantic, his impoverishment was his plenitude. Surrendering to it was more a challenge to his quickly shifting moods than the timeworn advice he had been receiving from his co-workers who sought to better their ways through conspiracy.

THE SOUL AND POVERTY

Rollo May (1983) has cited Nietzsche in pointing to the soul's way of overcoming its limitations. "The spirit grows," wrote Nietzsche, " . . . (and) strength is restored by wounding" (p. 81).

Certainly it is not popular to conceive of the potency of an expanding wounded system. Nevertheless, the poor are society's throbbing unconscious. Elvin's shifting moods were his attempts at making contact with his underlying forces of survival. The "down" moods could have brought him no lower. In a seemingly perverse mode, they protected him against the terrors of annihilation. The "ups" were rich in their ability to grant "rich" pleasures. Together, and only at rare moments, both moods combined in interdependence. The resulting quality allowed Elvin to experience a personal affirmation of his participation in the life of the larger community.

"I'm able to feel a lot better when I flip into not feeling so poor that I'll starve."

"Try to capture that sense of yourself," I requested. "Can you describe it for me?"

"It's like I'm having my own way. . . . If I were all loaded down with responsibility I could never have made it. That's just me. No one else. Other people can have a lot they're dependent on. That's just not my way. But when I feel OK, it's like I belong to most of the world."

Elvin's therapy ended with many new options. He was able to choose a new route in his job. He began to understand that his richness was a direct result of his "traveling light." He has kept in contact with me and, according to him, with two or three "steadies." We were, according to him, "the guardians of his soul."

POVERTY AND EMOTIONAL FULFILLMENT

There is a link between poverty and emotional and social fulfillment, though, more often than not, poverty evokes fears that life has its heavy penalties. Yet, it is also true that life for the poor has, as it were, its own rewards. Ernest Becker (1975) has said that "prosperity . . . (is the) universal ambition" (p. 3). In his way,

Becker sees prosperity as offering the hope of continuity. But such prosperity is only rich for the meaning each individual gives to his or her life. Elvin, like Tevye and like the martyr Simone Weil, articulates a certain wealth. They are themselves exemplars of non-prosperity. Elvin was delighted to be able to move on, in his words, "without a trace." Even his quick-shifting moods were his signs that inner unity could only be appreciated within his engagement with the necessary values in his life. Were he actually to become the "rich man" Tevye dreamed of being, the loss might have been too great.

REFERENCES

Becker, E. (1965). *Escape from evil*. New York: Free Press.
May, R. (1983). *The discovery of being*. New York: Norton.

Power and Poverty in Psychotherapy

Jorge A. Montijo

SUMMARY. There is no great distinction between psychotherapy with the poor and psychotherapy in general, just as the presumption of therapy's insulation from general social forces is also false. Precisely, therapy with the poor can help to understand critical issues that are present not only in therapy but potentially in every human interaction: domination, prejudice, oppression, and the limited possibilities for individual empowerment and liberation. This article stresses the importance of substituting the poor/affluent dichotomy for a dialectical analysis that contemplates the "poverty" or relative powerlessness of the more affluent therapists, together with the inherent capacity for empowerment and liberation in the dispossessed. Therapists' unrelenting analysis of themselves within therapeutic relationships and of social forces impinging upon the participants seems crucial for power-enhancing interventions.

Issues of power usually come to the fore in the treatment of poor patients (Bart, 1974). However, my contention is that domination, inequality, oppression, violence, powerlessness, submission, and empowerment are universal human occurrences that should be part of any analysis of therapeutic interaction but are mystifyingly omitted in most instances. The purpose of the present article is to explore oppression and empowerment as dialectical and universal phenomena in psychotherapy by focusing on the therapeutic relationship with poor patients as point of departure.

Even though psychology is broadly described as the science of human behavior, and encompasses in its field of study reflex re-

Jorge A. Montijo, PhD, Adelphi University, 1974, is a practicing health psychologist specializing in clinical neuropsychology. The author is grateful to Dr. Enrique N. Arsuaga for his helpful suggestions in the preparation of this article. Mailing address: Ponce de León 623, Office 1106, Hato Rey, Puerto Rico 00917.

sponses to psychic phenomena, it has not eagerly pursued politically charged constructs, such as structural and institutional violence, oppression, and liberation processes (Bulhan, 1985). Instead, political and critical analyses are restricted to individual proponents, such as Bulhan (1985), Beit-Hallahmi (1974), Halleck (1971), Hurvitz (1973), and Ryan (1976); or to so called "activist" groups, such as gay and lesbian psychologists, feminists, and certain sectors of community psychology.

The evident discrimination against the poor and other oppressed minorities best provides a source of critical analysis in psychology. The extremity of these conflicts prevents the assumption of a benign or even neutral societal response. Also, researchers in these areas very often have been or are themselves the victims of discrimination and heightened oppression.

In his book *Blaming the Victim*, Ryan (1976) proposed that dominant ideology tries to justify poverty, discrimination, and social injustice by locating the source of evil within the sufferers themselves, thus exonerating prevailing social structures and practices. Bulhan (1985) has documented the prevalence of racial and socioeconomic prejudice among the pioneers of academic psychology, many of whom strongly believed in the intellectual and moral superiority of Anglo-Saxons and Northen Europeans over other ethnic groups, who conveniently would provide the former with cheap labor. Therefore, a psychological practice grounded on a Weltanschauung that interprets social inequality and injustice as a natural manifestation of human differences should often be inimical to the same opposed groups it pretends to help.

Modern psychodynamic therapy was born into the Viennese upper class. It has undergone numerous transformations since, and has intended to help populations for which it was not originally developed. The results of such efforts are generally recognized as highly favorable (Bergin & Lambert, 1978), leading some researchers to proclaim therapeutic practice a highly beneficial human activity (Smith, Glass, & Miller, 1980). Among the more than 250 different schools of psychotherapy, I personally favor those committed to a search for truth and self-discovery, in contrast to others that seem to seek results by any means, including deception. In my opinion, therapeutic effectiveness is maximized by a strict analysis of patient-therapist interaction, including its political parameters and social determinants. By and large, such analysis is not a part of customary clinical practice. An examination of the therapeutic relationship with poor patients provides an opportunity to explore this general concern.

IDEOLOGICAL COMPLICATIONS IN THERAPY WITH THE POOR

The use of special therapeutic approaches with the poor has been frequently proposed (Acosta, Yamamoto, & Evans, 1982; Dudley & Rawlins, 1985; Lorion, 1978; Prince, 1969; Rivera, 1984). However, Evans (1985) has warned of the dangers of "activist-oriented, content-focused curricula in isolation from traditional theory, knowledge and skills" in the training of therapists for black populations (p. 457). The need to recognize both human universality and group and individual differences in therapeutic practice has been implicitly or explicitly acknowledged by many researchers and practitioners (Dudley & Rawlins, 1985).

In my opinion, a dialectical rather than a dualistic analytical method holds the key to a better understanding of therapeutic processes in general, and of the vicissitudes of therapy with the poor in particular. Fanon (1968) has characterized the ideology of colonization as Manichean: The colonizer represents good, wealth, and power, whereas the colonized represents evil, need, and powerlessness. A dialectical method and particularly his interpretation of Hegel's master-slave paradigm (Bulhan, 1985) permitted Fanon to conceptualize colonialism as a struggle between basically similar human beings whose main difference is their degree of power.

When practiced incorrectly, therapy can resemble the colonization process: Therapists behave as if they are more powerful, knowledgeable, and mentally healthy than their patients, who are presumed to need the therapist as the slave needs the master. Such an extreme position is obviously countertransferential in a broad sense and may be considered unusual or extreme, but my experience is that it is commonly manifested to some degree. Therapy with the dispossessed, either economically or emotionally, is most likely to elicit such colonialist attitudes.

As members of society, therapists as a whole share its ideology (Bulhan, 1985; Navarro, 1981; Sarason, 1983). As mentioned, such ideology justifies inequality and oppression by presenting poverty as determined by personal defects of the poor. Similar arguments have been employed to justify colonialism and slavery (Bulhan, 1985; Fanon, 1968; Marqués, 1972; Memmi, 1972). The therapeutic enterprise almost by definition makes patients responsible for their condition. Typically, therapists and their patients ignore the social forces that largely determine their behavior and status, and seek to find the road to meaningful change strictly in their relationships. Such extreme denial of social determinants can border on the delusional (Lichtman, 1982), and its inappropriateness is nowhere more obvious than in the therapy of poor people.

In treating poor patients, therapists must quickly make a choice: Either they accept the determinant role of the social system in producing the need they are faced with, or they accept dominant ideology and classify such problems as strictly behavioral, interpersonal, or intrapsychic. The latter choice can lead to a reproduction of the dominant-oppressed dialectic in the therapy itself, and the results may often be anti-therapeutic. If the social forces that produce economic injustice can be ignored by therapists, they may in effect deny a nuclear experience of their poor patients and thus cut off all bridges to relationship.

FOSTERING THE THERAPEUTIC RELATIONSHIP

Acceptance of behavioral, interpersonal, or intrapsychic difficulties as primarily epiphenomena of larger social conflicts (Lichtman, 1982) is the first step in a difficult search for reciprocal recognition among therapists and poor patients. However, this awareness should not deny the presence and meaning of clinical symptoms (Evans, 1985). The aim of psychotherapy is to alleviate the suffering of specific human beings. Traditional psychodynamic approaches have proven helpful with poor patients. The relationship between egalitarian attitudes on the part of therapists and such success (Lerner, 1972) should help dispel the myth that poor patients can only be helped by directive, authoritarian means (Garfield,

1978; Lorion, 1978), or by the mystification inherent in folk practices (Prince, 1969).

As mentioned, successful therapy with the poor depends primarily on the quality of the therapeutic relationship (Montijo, 1985). Comas-Díaz and Minrath (1985) have discussed the danger of projective identification, as therapists may easily perceive their "bad self" in unsuccessful, impoverished patients. Such countertransferential tendencies can best be averted by the therapists' recognition and acceptance of their own relative neediness and powerlessness vis-à-vis dominant social forces.

Even if therapists regard askance the suggestion that they are personally needy or poor, their impotence in solving their dispossessed patients' problem in living is sheer reality. Therapy is a poor recourse against poverty and structural violence (Bulhan, 1985), and the recognition of this therapeutic powerlessness should help to build empathy and communication between common sufferers.

After taking this crucial step, therapists may find that they are not faced with passive, submissive, or merely resistant patients but rather with active participants and planners in matters affecting their destiny (Bart, 1974). Within every slave beats the desire to overcome and substitute the master (Fanon, 1968), and poor people do not resign themselves to their condition. Their resistance may take pathological forms but, like most psychopathology, it carries a message of protest and rebellion. Rather than judge, therapists should attempt to understand the relationship between social oppression and the pathology they are faced with, and reflect on their own condition. A more egalitarian, respectful, and helpful relationship may develop (Montijo, 1985).

CONCLUSION

Therapeutic effects are largely determined by the system that allows its practice. It is in no way a revolutionary activity, and its primary effect is most probably heightened adaptation to existing social conditions (Bulhan, 1985; Lichtman, 1982). However, the alleviation of human suffering seems to be a universally acceptable endeavor. Also, the manner in which psychotherapy is practiced — more democratic and less authoritarian and prejudiced — is itself a protest against prevailing social conditions, and a glimpse of a better future. As Beavers (1977) has noted, therapist functions run the gamut from control and coercion to the promotion of growth, and growth is best promoted in those social environments which are most respectful of their members' needs. Everyone needs power and heightened control over personal circumstances, and the emotionally and economically indigent are the most needy. When therapists monopolize power, they reproduce the social order in their consulting room, and are thus detouring therapy in process and direction. When they share power and, even more, face their own relative powerlessness, therapists promote empathy, community, and personal growth.

REFERENCES

Acosta, F. X., Yamamoto, J., & Evans, L. A. (1982). *Effective psychotherapy for low-income and minority patients*. New York: Plenum Press.

Bart, P. B. (1974). Ideologies and utopias of psychotherapy. In P. M. Roman and H. M. Trice (Eds.), *The sociology of psychotherapy* (pp. 9-57). New York: Jason Aronson.

Beavers, W. R. (1977). *Psychotherapy and growth: A family systems perspective*. New York: Brunner/Mazel.

Beit-Hallahmi, B. (1974). Salvation and its vicissitudes: Clinical psychology and political values. *American Psychologist, 29*, 124-129.

Bergin, A. E., & Lambert, M. J. (1978). The evaluation of therapeutic outcomes. In S. L. Garfield and A. E. Bergin (Eds.), *Handbook of psychotherapy and behavior change* (2nd ed., pp. 139-189). New York: John Wiley.

Bulhan, H. A. (1985). *Frantz Fanon and the psychology of oppression*. New York: Plenum Press.

Comas-Díaz, L., & Minrath, M. (1985). Psychotherapy with ethnic minority borderline clients. *Psychotherapy, 22*, 418-426.

Dudley, R. M., & Rawlins, M. R. (Eds.). (1985). Psychotherapy with ethnic minorities [Special issue]. *Psychotherapy, 22*. (2S).

Fanon, F. (1968). *The wretched of the earth*. New York: Grove Press.

Garfield, S. L. (1978). Research on client variables in psychotherapy. In S. L. Garfield and A. E. Bergin (Eds.), *Handbook of psychotherapy and behavior change* (2nd ed., pp. 191-232). New York: John Wiley.

Halleck, S. L. (1971). *The politics of therapy*. New York: Science House.

Hurvitz, N. (1973). Psychotherapy as a means of social control. *Journal of Consulting and Clinical Psychology, 40*, 232-239.

Lerner, B. (1972). *Therapy in the ghetto*. Baltimore: Johns Hopkins University Press.

Lichtman, R. (1982). *The production of desire*. New York: Free Press.

Lorion, R. P. (1978). Research on psychotherapy and behavior change with the disadvantaged. In S. L. Garfield and A. E. Bergin (Eds.), *Handbook of psychotherapy and behavior change* (2nd ed., pp. 903-938). New York: John Wiley.

Marqués, R. (1976). *The docile Puerto Rican*. Philadelphia: Temple University Press.

Memmi, A. (1965). *The colonizer and the colonized*. New York: Orion Press.

Montijo, J. A. (1985). Therapeutic relationships with the poor: A Puerto Rican perspective. *Psychotherapy, 22*, 436-440.

Navarro, V. (1983). Work, ideology and science: The case of medicine. In V. Navarro and D. Berman (Eds.), *Health and work under capitalism: An international perspective* (pp. 11-38). New York: Baywood Publ. Co.

Prince, R. (1969). Psychotherapy and the chronically poor. In J. C. Finney (Ed.), *Culture change, mental health and poverty* (pp. 121-154). Lexington: University of Kentucky Press.

Rivera, A. N. (1984). *Hacia una psicoterapia para el puertorriqueño* (Towards a psychotherapy for Puerto Ricans). Río Piedras, Puerto Rico: CEDEPP.

Ryan, W. (1976). *Blaming the victim* (rev. ed). New York: Vintage Books.

Sarason, S. (1981). *Psychology misdirected*. New York: Free Press.

Smith, M. L., Glass, G. V., & Miller, T. I. (1980). *The benefits of psychotherapy*. Baltimore: Johns Hopkins University Press.

On Being a "Poor" Psychotherapy Patient

Kaisa Puhakka

SUMMARY. This article examines the predicament of impoverishment which is distinguished from the economic condition of poverty. The former refers to a diminished way of being, doing, and having in the world that results from the identification of the self with "not having anything" and "not having it in oneself to have." This article maintains that the impoverished self's ability to engage in exchange is impaired and that this impairment lies at the root of other self-esteem issues, and needs to be addressed in therapy before other issues are addressed. How the therapeutic conditions can be set up so as to restore the patient's ability to engage in exchange is discussed.

POVERTY VS. IMPOVERISHMENT

The word "poor" means "not having things" as in the case of people who live in economic poverty. It can also mean "not doing something well" as in the case of a poor job performance. Finally, it can mean "not being well" as in the case of a poor old dog who deserves our pity. All of these meanings are connected, and all are relevant to the predicament of the poor patient in the psychotherapeutic encounter. Thus the equivocation of the meaning of "poor"

Kaisa Puhakka, MA in philosophy and PhD in experimental psychology from the University of Toledo, is a clinical psychologist, formerly Director of Consultation and Education at Court Diagnostic & Treatment Center, now in private practice in Toledo and also Adjunct Clinical Assistant Professor of Psychiatry at Medical College of Ohio. She received a postdoctoral diploma in clinical psychology from the Derner Institute of Advanced Psychological Studies, Adelphi University, in 1983. Mailing address: 6924 Springvalley Dr., Suite 220, Holland, OH 43528.

in the title of this article is not accidental but reflects something about the multifaceted nature of poverty, namely, that a person who *is* poor also tends to *feel* poorly and *do* poorly in whatever endeavors he or she undertakes, including psychotherapy.

Indeed, research generally suggests that low socioeconomic status is not conducive to being a good psychotherapy patient. Compared to their more fortunate peers, people from lower socioeconomic backgrounds tend to be less intelligent (Humphreys, 1985; McKenzie, 1984), have lower self-esteem (Hare, 1981), and are more susceptible to mental disorders (Albee, 1977; McSweeny, 1977). They tend to have more disruptive family lives and authoritarian child-rearing practices, whereas the research suggests that stable, well-functioning family life and non-authoritarian, open, and accepting child-rearing practices are conducive to higher levels of adult ego development (Dubow, Huesmann, & Eron, 1986; Looney & Lewis, 1983). Poor people are also seen by mental health professionals as having a poorer self-concept and prognosis than people who are economically better off (Sutton et al., 1986). And finally, they are less likely to seek help from psychotherapy even if such help is offered to them free of charge (Albee, 1977).

The meaning of "poverty" is complex, with multitudes of economic, cultural, social, and psychological dimensions. How one defines it depends on which of these dimensions is emphasized, in reference to what society poverty is defined, and also what kind of criteria are used, for example, an absolute standard of deprivation or the level of participation in or access to the exchange within the community (Rein, 1970; Townsend, 1987). Obviously not all low-income Americans feel impoverished or denied access to the "American Dream." And certainly, not all economically poor people are poor candidates for psychotherapy, even though the reality of their poverty presents special challenges to the therapist (Karon & Vandenbos, 1977).

This article addresses a phenomenon which, though not manifested by every economically poor person and sometimes manifested by persons living amidst material plenty, is most frequently encountered in psychotherapy with persons from the lowest socioeconomic strata. These persons may have subsisted on welfare for years, perhaps generations. They seldom come to psychotherapy of their own initiative but are usually referred by the courts, child protective services, and other community agencies. Because of their Medicaid benefits and involvements with other community agencies, they have an easier access to psychotherapy than do the relatively well-functioning working poor. Indeed, some are veterans of the community mental health system, having gone through the circuit of clinics, state hospitals, and often also the jails and probation departments. But as already mentioned, the phenomenon is not limited to these people but is sometimes encountered in people who are financially well off.

The phenomenon in question is the predicament of emotional and spiritual impoverishment that occurs when a person in a deeply existential sense identifies with being poor. It is important to note that the existential and psychological dimensions of impoverishment to be discussed in this article do not refer to "personality" or "personality traits." It is at least arguable that some personality traits are genetically inherited, but no such possibility exists for "impoverishment" as this condition is understood in the present context. Unlike a personality trait, impoverishment is not necessarily an enduring, or relatively enduring, part of the person's psychological make-up. It can be alleviated and even eliminated with the restoration of the person's self-experience. On the other hand, impoverishment can be more enduring than a personality trait, and it can be passed on through generations in entire families, perhaps entire communities. The term predicament is used because it connotes a condition into which one has fallen and by which one is deeply affected. Individuals who identify with being poor and thus have fallen into the predicament of impoverishment can display other personality traits as well. But it is the predicament of impoverishment and its associated self-experience, apart from other personality characteristics of individuals, that is the subject of this article. The purpose of this article is to explore the phenomenology of impoverishment and the unique challenge that the impoverished self presents to psychotherapy. Our thesis is that the understanding of the predicament of impoverishment and its addressing *at the outset* of therapy is necessary if the therapy is to have any measure of success.

THE PREDICAMENT OF IMPOVERISHMENT

The impoverished person's self-experience is characterized by a profound sense of lack or want. This "lack" or "want" is so profound as to possess an ontological dimension not encountered in the more common experiences of lack of some particular object or attribute, as when a person lacks a trade, a skill, a wife, or a car. The latter experiences are usually associated with a felt need to replenish the lack and an attendant anxiety about acquiring what one lacks. One thus feels the need to have what one doesn't have, or doesn't have enough of. Erich Fromm (1976) has characterized the preoccupation with "needing to have" and "needing to have more" as living in the *having mode*. Fromm considers this mode, illustrated by the values of an acquisitive consumer society, as inferior to living in the *being mode*, which is characterized by creativity, self-expression, and active engagement in exchange with the world. Fromm's *being mode* is associated with a sense of fulfillment, of "having enough," whereas the *having mode* is associated with a sense of insufficiency and "not having enough"; hence the anxious need to have more.

The fundamental conviction that one is incapable of having anything at all, that "I don't have it in me to be, do, or have anything," forfeits the need to have more and also frees the person from anxiety. Such a conviction is usually not an object of conscious experience. But it can reach to the very core of one's self-identity and become a condition one identifies with without being conscious of it. As such, it can become a powerful determinant of one's behavior as well as of experience of self and world (Puhakka & Hanna, 1988). The identification of the self with being "not capable of having anything" is what constitutes the predicament of impoverishment or impoverished self-experience. The defining characteristic of this kind of self-experience is incapacity to *have*, rather than not having some particular thing or attribute.

Heidegger's term *Dasein* ("Being-there") conveys the active, here-and-now connectedness with the world that characterizes the way living beings, including humans, are. For Heidegger (1962), "care" is the ontologically fundamental condition of *Dasein*:

That by which this entity [*Dasein*] is cleared—in other words, that which makes it both 'open' for itself and 'bright' for it-self—is what we have defined as 'care,' in advance of any 'temporal' interpretation. In care is grounded the full dis-closedness of the 'there.' Only by this clearedness is any illu-minating or illumining, any awareness, 'seeing' or *having something* [italics added] made possible. (pp. 401-402)

Heidegger equates care ontologically with human existence (*Da-sein*). As such, it is more fundamental than, and renders possible, the attitude of caring as well as its opposite, being care-free (p.84). When addressing *Dasein*'s possible ways of being-in-the-world, Heidegger uses a closely related term, usually translated as "con-cern."

Ordinarily, a person who does not care about something is inter-ested in or preoccupied with something else—cares about some-thing else. The proclamation, "I don't care!" acquires its assertive power precisely from such a contrast. Impoverished persons are not likely to proclaim their lack of care, because they *truly do not care about anything*. The loss of care simply manifests in the diminished way they are in relation to self and world alike. Thus it appears that the basic ontological condition that Heidegger describes as care is at issue with the impoverished person: Care can be distorted, dimin-ished, or lost touch with, at a level that is more profound than the conscious attitude of "caring" or "not caring" about a particular thing or person, including caring about oneself.

The loss or diminishment of care is illustrated by the welfare patient who was sent to psychotherapy by a children's protective agency when she was about to lose custody of her four children. She had lived, on and off for the past 13 years, with a man who did not support her and who had fathered two of her children. He was now accused of abusing the children physically and sexually, and she had filed domestic violence charges against him on occasion in the past. Commenting on her predicament, she said with a sigh that, given her evident sadness, had an oddly disingenuous ring to it , "I know I should leave him and I knew it a long time ago. I'd leave him now, if I only knew how." The disingenuousness of this pa-tient reflects her profound conviction that she is incapable of having whatever it takes to leave the abusive man and that therefore, her stated wish to the contrary, she knows she will not leave him.

When the impoverished self views itself as an object of awareness, "having nothing" and "not having it in me to have" are ways in which the self appears to itself. But the self who so views itself is uncaring in the radical and existentially profound sense discussed above. The painfully anxious feelings of inadequacy reflect one's openness to the possibility of having self-confidence, thus the intactness of one's basic care or concern. The welfare patient referred to earlier displayed no anxiety or despair about her predicament. Her evident sadness and even anger notwithstanding, she conveyed little concern or care. However, if asked whether she cared, she would not know to say "no." The problem is not the impoverished person's refusal to care about things that should be important to him or her. Rather, the problem is the person's foreclosure of the possibility of having or doing, or being anything. This foreclosure can be so radical as to leave the person entirely free of anxiety or defiance. When having, doing, or being something is no longer considered a possibility, the care and concern which nurture this possibility and which in turn are inspired by it also die.

ATTRIBUTES OF THE IMPOVERISHED SELF

Having explored the predicament of impoverishment, we shall now turn to the two major attitudinal and behavioral manifestations of this predicament. These are chronic complaining and apathy.

Even when the self has resigned itself to "not having it" in itself to have, do, or be anything, a sense of a lost possibility may still linger. The impoverished person is mourning a loss, often conveyed through incessant complaining and attempts to draw pity from the listener. The complaining patient who only wants pity and rejects all offers of help is all too familiar to psychotherapists. Behind the myriad "surface" complaints such a patient is mourning for the lost possibilities of his or her impoverished self. Every helpful suggestion by the therapist is seen as "impossible" and rejected; every effort by the therapist to bring about positive changes more directly is sabotaged. For the patient is convinced that any change in his or her situation will only result in further loss and want. The therapist wants the patient to get rid of his or her problems, but an impoverished patient is convinced that problems are the only things he or she "has" and consequently is unwilling to give them up. The only kind of "help" the patient can accept is sympathy or pity.

Many impoverished persons have given up mourning their loss altogether and are in a state of indifference or apathy. On the surface such psychotherapy patients can be cheerful, congenial, and entertaining, as they are not averse to distractions from their basic apathy. But, most of all, they are complacent. The complacency of the apathetic patient who has everything wrong in his or her life but is much less upset about it than the therapist is a familiar source of frustration encountered in psychotherapy with impoverished patients.

The impoverished person is often described as being "resistant" to psychotherapy. This, I believe, can be misleading. For "resistance" in therapy usually involves a conflict of wills, either within the patient or between the patient and the therapist. As an expression of will, resistance is basically healthy, even if perhaps misguided and maladaptive, and as such can be turned to therapeutic benefit. However, in the impoverished patient, resistance represents a failure of will. This is particularly the case with the apathetic patient. Such a patient brings into the therapeutic situation an impassivity that has a solid, heavy quality with no possibility of movement. The patient who is a chronic complainer still possesses some will, but it is diffuse and lacks direction; any change, which the patient perceives as being something that is imposed on him or her, is resisted. This bears a superficial resemblance to the passive-aggressive resistance through which some psychotherapy patients express their need for control. But the impoverished patient's issue is not one of control. Whether constantly complaining or apathetic, the impoverished patient simply does not have it in him or her to engage in a therapeutic exchange.

THE IMPOVERISHED SELF
AND THERAPEUTIC EXCHANGE

The experience of the therapist who tries to help the impoverished person can be much like tossing things into a bottomless well:

One can keep tossing things in, but nothing ever comes out, not even the sound of a splash or a thump indicating that something was received. The impassivity of the impoverished patient can be merciless to the therapist intent upon helping the patient.

The sense of defeat that accompanies the therapist's attempt to help is inevitable, because the impoverished self is not in a position to receive help. Receiving anything involves reaching out, opening up, and taking in what is offered. The impoverished self is not a participant in such an active process; things "happen to" or are "done to" the impoverished self. While the therapist may feel that he or she is "doing for" the poor patient and the patient may superficially agree with the therapist about this, at an existentially more basic level of self-experience, the patient is being "done to." When the therapist implicitly agrees with the patient's conviction about his or her self and assumes the position of a "helper," the result is a pernicious game in which the patient becomes increasingly helpless and downgraded and, paradoxically, more powerful in his or her weakness while the frustrated therapist who presumably has all the knowledge and power is rendered impotent. Kuntz, Clingaman, and Soper (1987) offer an insightful analysis of this helping game and contrast it with healing in which positive changes result from a genuine dialogue. As these authors observe,

> The healing experience appears to occur when the helper and the helped are unaware of differences in weakness and power and meet one another in the 'zone of equality' that is bound by the openness and vulnerability of one to the other. (p. 214)

In the encounter with the impoverished patient, this "zone of equality" needs to be restored before any kind of therapeutic exchange is possible. Such a restoration requires more than an affirmation, however empathetically conveyed, by the therapist of the basic equality of the therapist and patient as persons. For even when the therapist conveys his or her willingness to meet the patient in the zone of equality, the patient may not be willing or even able to do the same. The therapist must do more than affirm his or her own liberal view; he or she must explicitly disagree with the impoverished patient's implicit assumptions about self and world that constitute his or her predicament. The very conditions for the therapeutic relationship must reflect disagreement with this predicament. Thus, it is not enough that the therapist convey his or her expectation that the patient is an equal, capable of both giving and receiving in the therapeutic exchange. The therapist must initially go beyond merely conveying an expectation to actually implementing the conditions of equal exchange. For if expectations are conveyed without making sure that they are actually met in concrete, real terms, the therapeutic encounter is likely to further confirm the patient's impoverished self-experience.

The currency used in a restorative therapeutic exchange must be concrete, experientially real. For when the sense of having nothing to give infuses one's concrete, lived experience, it takes nothing less than a concrete, lived experience of "having something to give" to replenish one's impoverished self. The sliding-scale fee has been widely practiced as a solution to the exchange problem in the community mental health agencies that serve the poor. But, as Goldberg (1977) has noted, the very low fee which many poor patients can afford to pay is more symbolic than real. The therapeutic value of symbolic experiences lies in their power to evoke real emotional experiences which bring about the needed restructuring or reorganizing of a person's view of self and world. However, when the desired experiences are not within the patient's repertoire to be evoked, when the self needs restoration and replenishment in a very fundamental way, these experiences must be provided directly and concretely, "in the raw" so to speak.

Such restorative experiences can be provided by requiring the patient to donate his or her time and effort to helping others, for example, at a volunteer organization serving the patient's community, in return for the therapeutic services which the patient receives. A decade and a half ago, Goldberg and others noted the therapeutic significance of such arrangements to impoverished patients and also suggested ways in which these could be accomplished in a community clinic setting (Goldberg & Kane, 1974a; Goldberg & Kane, 1974b; Sata, 1972). Goldberg (1977) noted that he knew of only one other clinic besides the one in Maryland of which he was the director where the payment-in-kind method of compensating for psychological services had been implemented. It is my impression that the utilization of this method is no more wide-spread today than it was a decade ago. Goldberg (1977) noted the resistance from other community agencies to his barter system. Indeed, an implementation of such a system at the level of agency policy could amount to a mini-revolution with ramifications to the socioeconomic base of the community. It is not the job of the psychotherapist to carry out social-economic reforms or revolutions (even though the psychotherapist as a private citizen may have an active involvement in such endeavors). But the opportunities for service are not limited to those created by formal arrangements between agencies. Volunteer organizations, families, and neighborhoods offer unlimited informal opportunities for patients to become involved in caring for others and in giving of themselves.

The restorative effect of such involvement on the impoverished self can be dramatic, as illustrated by the following psychotherapy patient of mine. On and off welfare, this 25-year-old woman had a history of sporadic drug abuse, overdosing, suicidal threats and gestures, destructive relationships, and alienation from people who had been caring and helpful to her. She was chronically angry and full of contempt, especially toward those who tried to help her. Her defiance and contempt were conveyed in her affected masculine posture and gait as well as her wildly grotesque makeup which, when it was a topic of discussion in the therapy, was referred to as her "Indian war paint." When she lost her job and was unable to pay for her therapy, her acting out and attempts to sabotage the therapy increased. She was told that she is expected to donate two hours of her time at a volunteer service of her choice for each hour of psychotherapy she receives from me. Initially stunned by this new requirement, she then chose to work at a shelter for battered women. In the session following her first day at the shelter, she appeared a dramatically changed person. For the first time in the three years I had known her, her "Indian war paint" was gone, she walked softly and talked in a subdued voice. The following sessions were spent discussing her self-doubts and feelings of inadequacy about her ability to give, and the newly emerged feelings of warmth she was experiencing toward the women with whom she worked.

For this woman, as for many others, the experience of giving is restorative of the impoverished self. The newly emerging self is naturally very insecure and beset with painful feelings of inadequacy. But it is receptive to the therapist's support and encouragement in a way that an impoverished self who has nothing — not even enough to feel inadequate about — cannot be. It is at this point, not before, that a genuine therapeutic exchange can begin.

Engaging the patient to contribute from his or her resources is thus not the goal of therapy but the condition for therapy that is set up at the outset. In this way, the patient can enter into the therapeutic relationship as a person who can potentially experience himself or herself as being of equal worth with the therapist. Getting the patient to agree to this condition may take skillful effort and persuasion on the part of the therapist. The choice of a project that is relevant and within the means and resources of the patient is also important. But during the negotiations, especially if they are prolonged, the therapist should refrain from gratifying the patient's needs which brought him or her into therapy — in this way conveying to the patient the seriousness of the issue and, more importantly, that, regarding this issue, everybody is treated as equal.

CONCLUSION

Most people at some time in their lives encounter the experience of loss, as in the loss of a beloved person or treasured object. But when the loss deeply permeates one's self-experience, it is no longer a loss of a particular object but becomes a sense of not having, not being, and not being able to do anything at all. Such is the experience of impoverishment. The predicament of impoverishment deeply affects one's self-experience and relationships to others. In this article, an examination of this predicament was undertaken in order to shed light on some of its most difficult and intractable clinical manifestations. Among these, chronic complaining and apathy stand out as familiar to therapists. The chronic complaining or apathy of impoverished patients are characterized by an impassivity that seems to be far beyond the kind of psychological suffering that is active and alive — the kind that therapists feel they can work with. Therapists' attempts to help restore these patients' self-esteem by verbal encouragement, support, confrontation, or persuasion, however genuinely and empathetically delivered, often seem to be to no avail. This is because the impoverished person's ability to give and receive, to engage in any kind of exchange with other humans, is severely impaired.

This article maintains that in psychotherapy with the truly impoverished patient, it is the exchange between the patient and the world, not the patient's lack or want (e.g., of self-esteem), that needs to be addressed at the outset. Initially, the crucial difference between the patient and the therapist is that the therapist has faith in the patient's capacity for exchange whereas the patient lacks such faith. The therapist's faith must be reflected in the conditions of the therapy which provide an opportunity, in concrete, experiential terms, for the patient to give in return for the services he or she receives. A real experience of giving to others can restore one's self and bring about a new sense of having it in oneself to be and do things in the world one had previously believed impossible. With the dawning realization that "I have it in me" to be and do something, the time and effort expended and the personal risks taken begin to acquire value for the patient. When these things are offered in return for psychotherapy, the therapeutic exchange itself acquires value. Thus, a positive feedback system is activated which helps restore the self and its capacity to value, thereby enhancing the exchange between self and world which further enhances the self's connectedness with the world.

REFERENCES

Albee, G. W. (1977). Does including psychotherapy in health insurance represent a subsidy to the rich from the poor? *American Psychologist, 32*, 719-721.

Dubow, E. F., Huesmann, L. R., & Eron, L. D. (1986). Childhood correlates of adult ego development. *Child Development, 58(3)*, 859-869.

Fromm, E. (1988). *To have or to be?* New York: Bantam Books.

Goldberg, C. (1977). *Therapeutic partnership: Ethical concerns in psychotherapy* (pp. 209-232). New York: Springer Publishing.

Goldberg, C., & Kane, J. D. (1974a). Services-in-kind. A form of compensation for mental health services. *Hospital and Community Psychiatry, 25(3)*, 161-164.

Goldberg, C., & Kane, J. D. (1974b). A missing component in mental health services to the urban poor: Services-in-kind to others. In D. A. Evans & W. L. Claiborn (Eds.), *Mental health issues and the urban poor* (pp. 91-110). New York: Pergamon Publications.

Hare, B. R. (1981). Self-perception and academic achievement variations in a desegregated setting. In S. Chess & A. Thomas (Eds.), *Annual Progress in Child Psychiatry and Child Development*, (pp. 198-212). New York: Brunner-Mazel.

Heidegger, M. (1962). *Being and time*. New York: Harper & Row.

Humphreys, L. G. (1985). Race differences and the Spearman hypothesis. *Intelligence, 9(3)*, 275-283.

Karon, B. P., & Vandenbos, G. R. (1977). Psychotherapeutic technique and the economically poor patient. *Psychotherapy: Theory, research and practice, 14(2)*, 169-180.

Kuntz, G., Clingaman, J. G., & Soper, P. (1987). Helping and healing: The paradox of power and weakness. *The Humanistic Psychologist, 15(3)*, 208-214.

Looney, J. G., & Lewis, J. M. (1983). Competent adolescents from different socio-economic and ethnic contexts. *Adolescent Psychiatry, 11*, 64-74.

McKenzie, B. (1984). Explaining race differences in IQ: The logic, the methodology and the evidence. *American Psychologist, 39(11)*, 1207-1233.

Puhakka, K., & Hanna, F. (1988). Opening the POD: A therapeutic application of Husserl's phenomenology. *Psychotherapy, 25(4)*, 582-591.

Rein, M. (1970). Problems in the definition and measurement of poverty. In P. Townsend (Ed.), *The concept of poverty* (pp. 46-63). New York: American Elsevier Publishing.

Sata, L. S. (1972). A mental health center's partnership with the community. *Hospital and Community Psychiatry, 23*, 242-245.

Sutton, R. G., & Kessler, M. (1986). National study of the effects of clients' socio-economic status on clinical psychologists' professional judgments. *Journal of Consulting and Clinical Psychology, 54(2)*, 275-276.

Townsend, P. (1987). Conceptualizing poverty. In Z. Ferge and S. M. Miller (Eds.), *Dynamics of Deprivation* (pp. 31-44). Brookfield, VT: Gower Publishing.

Impoverishment in Therapy

Peter M. Rosenzweig

SUMMARY. This paper identifies the cycle of emotional impoverishment in therapy. It presents impoverishment as a natural lifelessness-helplessness which periodically affects both therapist and patient. The author's own experience and approach to impoverishment are presented. This approach can be best described as a combination of a dignified acceptance of personal limits and an emphasis on the therapeutic process as a potentially enriching "loan."

The School of Rabbi Ishmael taught: "There is a cycle (of poverty and means) that turns in the world."

Passing thoughts, if you will. I recall my surprise when a seemingly tight and dry supervisor told me that he always treated at least one patient of his case load pro bono. Images float by of the 1960s, ghetto patients seen in clinics for whom free therapy with me was both a sanctuary to release barely controlled rage and sadness, and a betraying prison where so much could be said but seemingly little done. I am reminded of once-poor patients who inflated my sense of goodness with their appreciation for token fees and who later fed my cynicism by not offering much back when good fortune placed them in mansions with views of the ocean. I smile at the simple dignity of a modern-day pack mule of an Irishman I once treated. He came to group one night announcing what was to me a therapeutically premature decision to leave treatment. After hearing my standard assurance that money is not a reason I accept for leaving therapy, he said simply, "This is not to put down your generosity,

Peter M. Rosenzweig, PhD, is a clinical psychologist in full-time private practice in Chicago. He is a member of the faculty of the Department of Clinical Psychology at Northwestern University. Mailing address: 713 Golf Mill Professional Building, Niles, IL 60648.

37

but it's about my dignity as a man with limits." These and other events combine with thought about the virtue and wisdom of charity and social-spiritual justice.

Yet, what I want to write about most is the experience of impoverishment in the therapy "hour." One way that therapy imitates life and is life for me lies in the mixture of poverty and richness. There are those moments when exchanges with my patients are enlivening, stimulating, satisfying, illuminating, and funny. Then there are the *others*: those that drain, deaden, and dull my vitality. From this perspective, poverty and therapy, whether literal or figurative, is about surviving life rather than living it.

It is a matter of irony that pain is the same agent that both forces us to survive and can liberate us from the cotton cocoon of survival. Roger is a poor patient of mine. He is an actor whom I see for a token fee. Roger, like so many other actors, spends much time out of work and struggles to make do with meager means. What sets Roger apart from other poor patients I've seen is the impoverishment we share together. Unlike some of the narcissistic, social nonconformists who act, Roger has little to say. His associations are unimaginative; even his complaints about the cold weather, the futility of therapy, and life are drab. His father's suicide, which took place when Roger was ten, hangs over the hour like the long black crepe that firemen hang outside firehouses to commemorate the death of their fellows. The poverty in one hour which I describe is a mixture of helplessness against the hand of fate; paralysis with the psychic pain of a lost, wasted father; and my own lack of inspiration.

Adele, too, is poor. Her physically and emotionally sick parents did not wait for old age to run out of gas. When she got excited somewhere in adolescence about the great void of caring in her life, they had her admitted to a hospital and calmed her modest protest with large doses of Thorazine. Adele, like Roger, does not cry or even attempt to mourn. She waits carefully at the outset of each session for me to betray her limited trust by terminating her therapy or suggesting hospitalization. I continue to see Adele every other week pro bono, but my attention wanders as I enter her environment of passive mistrust and unborn dreams.

I hate impoverishment. I loathe the ennui and lifelessness of surviving hours of my life in therapy. In earlier years, I would have drawn on my own anger and fear to thwart Roger and Adele's attempts to sweep me into the shame that finds me when I am helpless. Today I listened to Roger with active sensitivity. My reclarification of his words and my mindful avoidance of attributing feelings he does not experience, are the best of my craft and person. With Adele, I am different. Hours of patient listening for the rumblings of that "pre-Thorazine sprite" have begun to pay off. I gently tease the rage and sensuality hidden by apathy and inattentiveness. Life, at whatever level, flutters inside my hour with Adele; the tension of walking across a tightrope enlivens the work with Roger. Soon he will weep for his dad or choose with rage and indignation to continue his emotional suicide. Adele's eyes flirt with my insistence that a wealth is hidden behind her mistrust. Most importantly, I am alive again, having found a way to massage pain firmly and with direction.

I'm never sure whether impoverishment is a necessary part of "correct therapy" or lost/poor technique. The richness is in the dignity that comes with some measure of acceptance for clinical/personal limits, both mine and theirs.

In the Jewish tradition, the words poverty and tzedakah go hand in hand. Tzedakah, which is almost universally mistranslated as charity, actually means doing the right thing. The Talmudic explanation for the "rightness of tzedakah" is that by helping the poor one helps God, as it were, to balance social justice. Within that context, one who performs tzedakah is seen as quieting the poor man's complaint against God and ends his protests of the unfair advantage of the rich. Unfortunately, when treating the poor patient, one may find doing tzedakah difficult if not impossible. However well timed an interpretation might be, it does not nourish a starving patient the way a good meal may satisfy a hungry man. Pointing out self-defeating, self-impoverishing behavior, however well documented and clearly stated, offers little immediate relief.

However, as the Jewish ethic incites the therapist's dilemma it also offers a balm. The Talmud, in discussing tzedakah, deals not only with the outright sharing by giving. It also highlights the formulation of a partnership by way of making loans to the needy as being the most excellent form of tzedakah. The loan allows the poor their own options on success. Seen from this perspective, it is a process of partnership that enriches. Life can seep into those dead moments of surviving the hour, when the process, not the impediments or the goals, are at the center.

The last facet of poverty in therapy that catches my eye is solitude. The solitude that for me is such an inherent part of doing therapy is impoverishing. At times that solitude is imposed on me by the work. Patients will jettison me out of the flow so that they can attend more privately to their own suffering, helplessness, or triumphs. Sometimes, I find myself impoverished by the fact that privacy is such a part of being a confidential partner. Economic demands and a busy workload too often press me into forgetting the relief afforded by the fellowship of other therapists. Writing this piece has bridged that for now, and reminded me again of the richness of sharing by the written word and good company.

Poor People Can Make Rich Patients

Ronald E. Fox

SUMMARY. After making the general point that our views and attitudes toward the poor are a function of the personal and social environments within which we function, the author provides a brief personal context for understanding his own views, and then presents vignettes of five former patients that he has treated. Following the case vignettes, some simple lessons important to the author's development as a therapist are drawn in the hope that they may stimulate similar reflections in others.

It would not be difficult to make a case for the assertion that Western civilization has a long-standing ambivalent attitude toward the poor. There is the recurring idea, for example, that poverty is a disgrace or source of shame: "The poor man's wisdom is despised and his words are not heard" (Ecclesiastes 9:16). Conversely, there is the idea that poverty is somehow ennobling, as in Shakespeare's reference to a "poor but honest" man who can be trusted to be honest because he has nothing to lose. Having no earthly possessions of value, the poor are sometimes seen as more capable of attention to lasting human values. Another recurring theme in some religious, social, and ethical systems is the idea that the more fortunate have a moral obligation to help those who are less fortunate: "He that hath pity upon the poor lendeth unto the Lord" (Proverbs 19:17). Many other examples come to mind but they would not change the point that the poor have always been with us and we have never been sure what to think about or to do with them.

Ronald E. Fox, PhD, University of North Carolina at Chapel Hill, 1962, has been Professor and Dean, School of Professional Psychology, Wright State University, since 1977. Mailing address: School of Professional Psychology, W.S.U., Dayton, OH 45435.

Reflecting the culture in which we are embedded, it seems to me that psychologists show a similar ambivalence to clients who are poor. On the one hand, we have adopted professional standards that encourage us to "provide some services to individuals or organizations for little or no financial return" (APA 1981); but it is my impression that many of my colleagues believe that people value only that which they earn or pay for and that patients who pay nothing are unlikely to be motivated enough to see long-term therapy through to completion. While I do not have the figures immediately at hand, the last time I looked it seemed clear that poorer patients tend to receive more serious diagnoses and are less likely to be recommended for individual psychotherapy than patients with good financial resources. I am well aware that such data are confounded (seriously disturbed people are unlikely to be able to hold a high paying job, etc.), but it remains my impression that many of us quickly begin thinking of alternatives to psychotherapy once we discover that a potential new client is poor.

It is not my intent to indict psychology or any other profession. Nor do I wish to belittle the amount of pro bono work that many of my colleagues provide each year. I simply wish to make the point that I think that we live and practice in a social environment that has an attitude toward the poor that is not always complimentary and frequently is patronizing, and that despite our posturing we share more of those attitudes than we sometimes dare to admit.

Over the 27 years that I have been practicing, I have seen some patients in psychotherapy who were extremely poor, probably at about the same frequency as many of my colleagues. The numbers are real but modest. I've never been at personal financial risk because of the large number of poor clients that I was seeing. As I search through my mental files for the relevant cases, a few come to mind as ones that were important to my continuing development as a psychotherapist and as a person. I am choosing to share them here in the hope that I will stimulate similar recollections in others and help make the point that contrary to F. Scott Fitzgerald's observation that the "rich are very different from us," the poor may not be so very different from us after all.

Before proceeding, a brief personal biographical note may help to provide a context for understanding my point of view. I came from a family that was poor and whose ancestors were poor as far back as anyone could remember. My father worked and improved his lot over the years so that by the time I was grown we properly could not be called poor anymore. But in the time I recall as my childhood, we were poor. In our small town, most of the population were poor aside from a few professional people, merchants, and manufacturers and one or two who were truly rich. I have an affinity, an affection really, for that small town and for the poor people who populated it. I still resonate to the down-home, easy familiarity that characterized life there. There was a constant sharing of the abundance (fresh or canned) from the omnipresent gardens, a readiness to help one's neighbors, and an abiding appreciation for the value of hard work. Though open and generous with friends, there was a marked suspiciousness of those who "put on airs" or seemed to think that they were better than others.

Being poor in that time and in that place was nothing to extol or praise. We knew that we were poor and we wanted not to be. But poverty came with a twist of wry. As one denizen put it: "I've never knowed anybody so poor but that they could afford to keep one dog. And I've knowed some so poor that they could afford to keep three." In a fit of frustration my grandfather once observed that "being poor is no disgrace but it sure is inconvenient as hell!" thus inadvertently providing humorous relief to family members for many years after when confronted with the hard reality of big dreams and little money.

I liked the people there and I wanted them to like me. So I never tried to "put on airs." After I went away to college, I sometimes acted less intelligent and educated than I was in order to be accepted. It was a source of pride to me that I could return home and be accepted as the same person unchanged by education. My penchant for speaking in the local argot, heavily laced with slang and poor grammar, persisted into graduate school and was evident in some of my clinical reports. It was a wise supervisor who managed to uncover the source of my act and to bother to understand the insecurity that motivated it. He enabled me to see that I had changed despite my wishes. I had learned things, acquired new skills, and in the process made myself something a bit different than I had been. He was the one who taught me that I could not deny what I had become any more than I could deny my roots. "You do not honor your heritage by acting ignorant or uneducated," he said. He was right of course. I gave up the act and found out that I was still accepted. What I had seen as anti-intellectualism I came to see somewhat differently. What is sometimes expressed as disdain for "egg-heads" may be just that; but it also may mask a rather timid insecurity. In such cases the unspoken question is not a sneer, "You think you're better than me just because you were lucky enough to go to college, don't you?" but a plea for human understanding ("Can you appreciate me, being so different? Can you reach across the gulf created by your education and your experience in a world I haven't seen to make contact with me? Do you really want to?").

Small towns populated with poor people still constitute my briar patch. I feel at home in them even 35 years after I left one. I'm still somewhat of an alien resident in the respectable suburbs and intellectual life of the upper middle class. It's not so much that I am afraid of being discovered for the poor redneck that I am and banished to my proper place, that seemed to go from me years ago; rather, it is that some things I cherish and value seem not to be found in the life that I've assumed. I seek a slower, smaller, quieter life in which I know the people with whom I live and work and play. I do not wish to be poor again, but I do not fear it. And I know that what I seek is overly idealized and nicer to remember than it was to live. Still, there was something about it worth recapturing. There were, and are, things to be learned there.

I have a comfortable sense of familiarity with the poor. Throughout my career I always have included at least one low-fee client in my case load at any given point in time. It is one way of paying some of my rent in the world.

My personal therapist was a man named Bingham Dai who was trained by Frieda Fromm-Reichman. It was Dai's belief that every patient would teach his or her therapist how to help them if the therapist would learn to listen appropriately. Applying his lessons to my own work, I discovered that patients not only could teach me about themselves, but they also helped me learn to be a better therapist for the next person. A few case vignettes in the next section will be used to illustrate some of the large and small things that I have learned from some of my low-fee clients.

CASE VIGNETTES

Case One

William was a middle-aged tenant farmer with five or six children who was referred by his family physician for help with a variety of somatic complaints that had no physical basis. He was desperately poor. As a tenant farmer he charged all seeds, fertilizer, groceries, clothing, and so on at a small shopping center owned by his landlord. Once crops were harvested and sold, the landlord received all of the cash and gave William's half to him in the form of credits to be used at the landlord's shopping center. Consequently, the only cash William ever saw were the small amounts that he or his family earned by performing small chores for others in the community. He once told me that he had not seen enough hard cash in the past 6 months to buy a bus ticket to the next town, a distance of about 50 miles. When he was a young man, William had an opportunity to take a "factory job" but had to turn it down because his father refused to help him borrow the small amount of money required to relocate and pay for food and shelter until his first paycheck arrived. He never forgave his father for that refusal. Nonetheless, he and his father continued to be close until the father's death about 3 years before he was referred to me. In the course of working through his unresolved anger and grief, William came to realize that he actually liked farming and the life it provided but that he did not have to continue working as a tenant for such an undesirable landlord. He found another arrangement nearby with more productive land and a more equitable financial arrangement. During the time that he was working through his grief, I encouraged him to visit his father's grave. He did so many times. At the end of our time together he asked that I go with him to the cemetery. I was hesitant but it seemed so important to William that I agreed. The cemetery was in a small churchyard on a low hill overlooking the bottom lands of a creek. The view was beautiful and peaceful. We sat by his father's grave and silently enjoyed the view for several minutes.

William explained to me how visiting his father's grave had helped him to really see the land that they both had loved and to remember some of the pleasant times that they had working together. He said that he also had learned something else from his visits and he wanted me to see what he was talking about: "When I sit here and see how beautiful the world can be, I begin to realize that there ain't none of it that is mine and yet all of it is ours." I saw what he meant.

Case Two

Sandy was a 15-year-old student referred by her teacher for a variety of symptoms that I no longer recall. What I do remember was that she was a bright, pretty, young woman who was trying to move out into the world of her peers, but was being stifled and held too close by her father. It was the father who proved to be the key person in my work with Sandy. In the beginning, he refused to give Sandy permission to see me or anyone else at the clinic. Despite what I had been taught about being a psychotherapist, I went to see the father and talked to him while he did his chores in the barnyard. Earl was a proud and stiff-necked farmer whose wife and daughter were being ground up by his bitter and unrelenting determination to conquer his few acres of the world and force it to release the comfortable living that he knew was in it. Austere, religious, principled, and unbending, he reminded me of the kind of characters described so well by Nathaniel Hawthorne. It turned out that a large part of his refusal to let his daughter come to the clinic was his inability to pay regular fees and his refusal to "accept charity." We arranged a barter system: milk, butter, eggs, and vegetables in exchange for my services. For several months I received precisely the correct amount of goods and produce, calculated at current market prices, sufficient to equal my customary fee. Shortly after I began seeing Sandy, I ran into her father at a local market. After a brief but meandering conversation he said, "Look, I know I'm not the easiest person to live with and I know that I'm not the best father in the world, but I do love my daughter and I never meant to hurt her. If you see anything I should do or change from your talks with her, then you just tell me what I should do and I'll do it." I did and he did. On several occasions, I sent him personal notes through Sandy telling him what I thought she needed from him and what I thought he should do about it. He came through like a prince every time. People take help in different ways. Some of us live by simple rules that may appear silly to others but that nonetheless may add meaning and value to an otherwise crushing reality. For all of his forbidding, uncompromising manner, I came to respect Earl. I still think of him on occasion when I start to wonder what it is I really stand for after all.

Case Three

Johnny was several months shy of his 16th birthday when he was sent to me for chronic truancy from school. Never a good student, Johnny had been "passed along" despite being absent for a large number of days each year. Now everyone seemed to be anxious for his next birthday to arrive so that he could drop out of school legally. Johnny's parents were intellectually limited, socially impoverished, mentally disturbed, and poor beyond description. With average intelligence and a few social skills, Johnny already was the shining star in his family. He had gone farther in school than any of them and, despite the many problems of his parents, he was a much beloved and overindulged son. One of his major problems, as I saw it, was that no one had ever loved him enough to say no. He was spoiled, arrogant, uneducated, overimpressed with himself, and eager to leave school so that he could get a car that would "outrun every cop in the county." The last was not a figure of speech, it was a goal that he actively pursued. I saw him for several weeks and although we seemed to take to each other nothing much happened. There seemed to be too little time, too little motivation, and too much to overcome. Finally, I decided to make my intervention around the school-attendance issue and told Johnny that I was going to insist that he attend school regularly until the required legal age. When he pointed out that he would learn nothing and that he would not be required to go to school after the age of 16, which was only 2 months away, I responded that the rule was that people had to attend school until the age of 16, not until they were almost 16. He objected but I did not relent. For the next week, I had the school principal call me when Johnny failed to show up. When that happened, I directed that an attendance officer go get Johnny and bodily take him to the principal. The principal, in turn, made sure that Johnny stayed in school the full day. Initially, the school personnel resisted my plans but gave in when I insisted that the purpose was not to teach Johnny spelling or geography but simply to help him learn that there are rules in the world that he must obey, even when he thought they were dumb. Further, I wanted him to experience having someone doing their best to help him even when it made him angry. When I saw Johnny the next week, he was furious with me. He called me a big bully (he was much smaller than the average) and lots of other unprintable names. He had a temper tantrum. Then he threatened to tear up my office. When I said that was unacceptable, he asked what would stop him. I pointed to my right bicep as I flexed it and said "Are you kidding? I'd take you easy and you'd better believe that I would. You try any rough stuff in here and I'll clean the floor with you like you was a mop!" Had he not been so small, I probably would not have been so confident! We glared at each other for awhile, then he said "You don't know what I'm like when I get really mad. If you would take me home to live with you for awhile then you would see how bad I really can be and you wouldn't be so sure of yourself." The last was said in a soft voice, almost a whisper in the calm following what had been a shouting, screaming tirade. I said, "I hear you John, but we can't do that . . . but I can see you the same time next week." We did continue to see each other and John did attend school. When he was 16 he dropped out with my blessings. He went to work with a painting contractor and he did buy a used car that looked to me very much like a hot-rod. We terminated our therapy sessions but for some time after Johnny would drop by at lunch time occasionally for a chat. We would grab a hot dog at the local bar, go for a brief stroll, and talk about his activities and his plans. I became something like an uncle or older brother to Johnny and he did OK. He is a painter. He is married. And he has a home and money in the bank. He did not try to outrun all the cops in the county. Lots of things can happen if you are willing to really intervene in someone's life . . . and sometimes it is necessary.

Case Four

Dan was brought to a local mental health clinic in a wheel chair on referral from his family physician following a week-long hospitalization that had failed to uncover any physiological basis for his symptom. The paralysis had occurred suddenly and mysteriously. He awakened one morning to discover that he was unable to move his legs. It turned out that the symptom was psychologically determined. Dan was the youngest and only male child in his family of origin. Since his parents had very much wanted a son after having three daughters, he was a highly valued addition to the family. From birth, Dan existed in an environment in which he was indulged, protected, and generally adored. His parents and sisters catered to him in almost every conceivable manner. At considerable sacrifice to his family, he became the first of them to complete high school. After graduating, he was able to obtain a job in the local furniture plant. Although it was a menial job, it was far better than anything his father had been able to do. Within another year or so, he married his high-school sweetheart and began a family of his own. With the help of his family and friends he was able to build a small home near where his parents lived. There was electricity but no running water. He was a good worker and received several promotions. After 10 years or so on the job, he was offered a supervisory position with the same company at a substantial salary increase but at a different plant in a city almost 100 miles away. Dan visited the plant and liked what he saw. Clearly the working conditions and the salary were superior to his current arrangement. The problem was that he would have to move to a city, and he would have to finally leave home. When he began to feel hesitancy about taking the job, he experienced a fair amount of guilt. He was a very religious young man and believed that he should seize any legitimate opportunity to better provide for his children. Also, friends heard about his good fortune and urged him to accept the new position. Faced with a choice between what he felt he should do and what he wanted to do, he went lame. That kept him from moving without having to feel guilty but it left him unable to walk. After a few sessions it became apparent that Dan was not going to be a candidate for any sort of psychotherapy aimed at uncovering the source of his conflict and resolving his dependency as I had learned to do. So, I reframed Dan's problem as a conflict between financial success and the quality of life he wanted for his children. Unable to choose because he was uncertain that his instinctive choice for the proper quality of life was correct and being so conscientious that he must do the right thing, he worried himself into a paralysis. He accepted my "analysis" of his problem and my strong admonition that he trust his instinctive choice and stop considering a move as the strain was "bad for his nerves." People talked like that in that time and place! "Going with the pathology" can sometimes help a person out of a difficult situation.

Case Five

Kate was brought to the family clinic of a large university medical center by her family for help with her "falling-out spells." Such "spells" were reported occasionally in rural areas to refer to a variety of ailments ranging from major seizures to something like a swoon accompanied by reports of feeling faint. The family stated that Kate would suddenly, and for no apparent reason, fall down and twitch. She did not injure herself when she fell, did not exactly lose consciousness but was not very responsive to questions or commands, and seemed to recover after several minutes of solicitous comfort and attention of various types. Kate was almost 15 years old when the "spells" began. She was brought to the family-therapy program after having made the rounds of the various other specialty clinics with no significant findings. The family was severely impoverished from every standpoint: economically, educationally, intellectually, and socially. The father managed a meager subsistence for his family through a combination of hunting, trapping, gardening, and hiring out as an occasional day worker. With seven children and a wife with several chronic ailments that I do not precisely recall, existence was strictly on a hand-to-mouth basis. Our initial assessment did not turn up very much that was useful in explaining Kate's "falling-out spells." I asked them to return "for further evaluation" without much hope of being able to find out anything useful or of being able to do much in any event. On the second visit, I discovered, almost accidently, that Kate still slept in the same bed with her parents. There did not appear to be any evidence of direct sexual abuse. Her parents were still sexually active. They usually waited until she was asleep before having sex but she sometimes complained that they woke her up. None of them seemed to think much about these events one way or the other. The situation was no different from how the parents had been raised. Sex was not a very private matter when people lived little differently from the early pioneers. I told them that I knew that they intended no harm but that we all knew how high-strung some young girls were and that it was not good for Kate's nerves to continue to sleep with her parents at her age. The parents accepted my advice and 6 weeks later there had been no recurrence of the spells that had been occurring at the rate of one every day or two. One should never overlook the obvious. When people live on a basic, survival basis, simple solutions may work wonders — particularly when proposed by a socially sanctioned authority.

A FINAL NOTE

There are no important or complicated lessons to draw from my experiences. A few simple principles emerged from experiences like these that proved useful to me and helped shape my practice over the years. I list them here for whatever use they may be to others.

1. Never underestimate the sensitivity and complexity of the human spirit nor the capacity of even the meanest of us to understand and to respond to the suffering of those we hold dear.
2. Remember that dignity, pride, and self-respect are not dispersed among people in accordance with their financial status.
3. Getting out of the office to engage people where they live and work is sometimes necessary.
4. It is not true that a monetary fee is required to convince people that therapy is valuable.
5. Do not disdain helping someone only a little bit when that is all that can be done at the moment. If you do no harm and help

only a little, it is likely that the patient will return for more help later on.

6. Do not give away your role as an authority too quickly, sometimes it may be the only tool you have with which to help someone.

I do not believe that the poor are all that different from other patients in the range of problems they present or what they need from me. Sometimes, I do need to be more flexible in how I proceed with such persons than is normally the case. Otherwise, I prefer to believe that we are all more human than otherwise. Finally, I would note that it is uncommonly difficult for me to work with any person or group that I do not respect, or for whom I feel sorry, or whom I am inclined to patronize. I believe that the same is probably true for other therapists as well.

REFERENCE

American Psychological Association. (1981). *Standards for providers of psychological services*. Washington, DC: Author.

Reduced Fee or Free Psychotherapy: Uncovering the Hidden Issues

Mary S. Cerney

SUMMARY. Nothing is free. We pay for everything, if not financially then psychologically, and that may be the higher price. Psychotherapy entails a price in time and money, a price people pay to change. The apparently simple issue of paying a fee masks complicated struggles that may remain untouched by therapy unless approached through discussion of the fee and its payment, particularly when the patient cannot pay the full fee. The author discusses issues related to payment of reduced fees, free treatment, and nonmonetary payment, illustrated with case examples. What, how, and when patients pay must remain a discussable issue throughout treatment.

Individuals enter psychotherapy to change some aspect of their lives that they find disturbing. Perhaps self-sabotaging behavior prevents them from using their own natural resources—their innate abilities—to better themselves, and repeated failures lower their already-damaged self-esteem. Tired of this downward cycle of failure and declining self-esteem, patients approach a therapist or clinic for help—only to find that they cannot pay the standard fee. There may be a sliding scale, but when, how, and with whom is it applied?

Dr. Mary S. Cerney is a Diplomate in Clinical Psychology, a graduate of the Topeka Institute for Psychoanalysis, a Senior Staff Psychologist at the Menninger Clinic, and Section Psychologist for one of the long-term units in the C. F. Menninger Memorial Hospital. She is a supervisor and member of the didactic faculty in the Karl Menninger School of Psychiatry and Mental Health Sciences, the Postdoctoral Program in Clinical Psychology; and she teaches in the Topeka Institute for Psychoanalysis. Dr. Cerney is Director of Grief Therapy and a supervisor and member of the Adult Psychotherapy Service where she does long- and short-term psychotherapy, hypnotherapy, grief therapy, and psychoanalysis. Mailing address: The Menninger Clinic, Box 829, Topeka, KS 66601.

In this paper I will address the problems that confront the therapist whose clients need and can use psychotherapy, usually on an outpatient basis, but cannot afford to pay the standard fee for treatment. The principles to be outlined here can also apply to the psychotherapy of individuals (including adolescents) whose treatment is financed by family, insurance companies, or other sources. These principles raise issues that need to be addressed even with individuals who do pay a standard fee. In this paper, I will not consider issues related to individuals who are hospitalized and so disorganized that they cannot hold a job. In that state, they probably cannot use a traditional psychotherapy.

THE MEANING OF MONEY

Krueger (1986a) states that money can be understood in several ways. It may be a vehicle for exchange of goods and services, a transference object, or a focus for examining attitudes and values. The issue of money, with its multiple theoretical and symbolic meanings, is so weighted with realistic and unrealistic implications that it is frequently just ignored and treatment is compromised or interrupted. Freud (1913/1958) once wrote: "Money matters are treated by civilized people in the same way as sexual matters—with the same inconsistency, prudishness and hypocrisy" (p. 131).

The issue of money is a complex of paradoxes. Money does not bring happiness, but we can be most unhappy without it. As Krueger (1984a) points out, "One who has a great deal of money is viewed as superior, yet the frank desire for money is considered poor taste or worse" (p. 4). For many therapists, asking for money is so distasteful that they can insist on payment only in crisis or anger. The manner in which they demand payment often destroys the treatment alliance. But allowing the bill to accumulate can have equally serious consequences. In one such case the court ruled that the therapist was at fault for allowing the bill to accumulate and the patient did not have to pay (*In re* H. Jon Geis, P.C. v. Landau, 1983). The psychological implications of such a situation are multidetermined and speak to problems within therapists, who end up poorer for all their effort, and to additional problems within patients, who must live with more guilt for "having gotten away with something." Matters become even more complicated when patients pay a reduced fee or are treated for free.

TREATMENT FOR A REDUCED FEE

Some therapists believe that they contaminate the therapeutic relationship by discussing such mundane issues as money. In reality they contaminate the relationship and compromise the treatment by *not* discussing financial arrangements, particularly reduced fees. A senior psychiatrist and I co-teach an introductory class on psychotherapy in which we stress the significance of the fee and how it can be a metaphor for many issues throughout treatment. We emphasize money as an issue that should not be slighted in the course of treatment. Yet in our supervision of third- and fourth-year residents, we rarely, if ever, find a resident who handles the issue of fee appropriately, despite the emphasis given to it in their second-year course. Somehow, in the course of their work, they forget this information or are uncomfortable discussing the bill and its payment.

Just as patients may feel unworthy of treatment and therefore be reluctant to pay their bill, so therapists — particularly beginners — may feel unworthy to charge for what they do. Many therapists fear their patients will think that they do not care for them if the fee is mentioned. Others may think they should be "above" having to deal with such issues. Charging a fee emphasizes that therapy is not a personal friendship but a business relationship and thus there is work to do. One patient said, "If I could meet you at the coffee shop over a cup of coffee, it would be so much easier to talk." When I asked what effect he thought such an informal meeting would have on the treatment, he conceded that it would probably sabotage it, and that he wouldn't be able to discuss the unpleasant aspects of treatment.

Case One: Self-Worth

If consistently and openly discussed throughout treatment, the issue of money can be one of the most important leverages to a successful treatment outcome. With the help of excellent supervision, a turning point in one of my early therapy cases centered on the issue of payment. Jack was paying a reduced fee through the outpatient clinic at a state hospital. He was quite negligent in paying and allowed his fee to accumulate despite our regular discussion about his accumulating bill. Prominent issues included Jack's feelings of self-worth, as well as questions he had about whether I cared, was I doing the therapy just because I needed a case, and would I stop seeing him if he didn't pay the fee.

After a lengthy exploration of whether he was worth the price of treatment and of his own feelings of worth, Jack admitted, "To pay for treatment would mean I'm also responsible for other aspects of my life. I would have to grow up." Jack was able gradually to bring his account up to date and to continue making regular payments on his bill. At that point, his treatment made a major turnaround. He was able to get a better job, and after much discussion, increased his payment schedule. When the issue of increasing payment was first raised, he threatened to terminate treatment and angrily accused me, "You are only interested in getting as much money from me as you can!" Underlying this reaction was his feeling of "getting away with something." Not paying a higher fee when he could afford it was damaging his sense of integrity. Discussion of this issue also initiated another major breakthrough in treatment. This individual, who could afford only a minimum fee at the beginning of treatment, ended treatment paying the standard fee. When he began treatment, he had difficulty holding a job for more than a month at a time; he is now a successful upper-middle-class businessman.

Case Two: Maintaining the Status Quo

Failure to pay and the consequent possibility of terminating treatment may be a patient's way of dealing with the wish to maintain the status quo, to avoid addressing painful issues.

> Tina had made significant changes since entering therapy. She had ended the abusive violence of her live-in boyfriend, and she had become more assertive in her day-to-day interactions. But paying her bill was still a problem. She explored this issue in therapy and interpreted for herself that not paying the bill showed how little she cared for her self and her own treatment.

She often commented that she was paying so little for her treatment. Others who could afford to pay the standard fee for treatment might benefit more.

Despite the patient's obvious understanding of what she was doing, her bill continued to mount. She readily loaned her available money to her boyfriend or others for little or no reason, and then she would come to therapy and berate herself for what she was doing. Tina searched for what she was afraid of learning—that her boyfriend was not right for her and she would have to leave him, or he would leave her. She feared if she continued to uncover hidden meanings she might find some dark secret in her past. Perhaps she had been raped or sexually molested and had no memory of it. She then added that her abuse of treatment by not paying was like a rape. As we examined both her wish to know and her fear of the consequences of revealing such information, the patient appeared to become more relaxed. Issues that had previously appeared so terrifying became less so when they were brought into the light of open discussion. Not paying the bill had many meanings. In the transference, I wasn't worth even the sum she paid and she wasn't worth any amount of money.

Changes in Tina's bill-payment behavior were minimal until we discussed that the bill would need to be made current or we would have to interrupt treatment until it was. At first, she strongly resisted this idea, but then related how her mother would rescue her from difficult circumstances. She explored the transference implications of my negotiation of a lowered fee for her. She then could begin to see how, by rescuing others and consequently forcing herself more deeply into debt, she was preventing others—her boyfriend and her family— from growing and assuming responsibility for their own debts.

FREE TREATMENT

Sometimes patients are unable to pay a fee at all for a time. For example, if a patient is in the hospital with no source of income, the insurance company and/or others may have to handle the fee payment. But having someone else pay the fee may solidify a sense of entitlement, that one is owed everything. Many patients have the attitude that "the world owes me a living. If I want something, I will take it, and if the other person doesn't like it, too bad." Having a third party pay a therapy fee can engender an attitude in the patient that "if I want something, regardless of what it is, I can have it and I can have it immediately." That attitude is detrimental to a treatment process that demands perseverance and the ability to tolerate delay of gratification.

Beneath this attitude, and more apparent in some individuals, is a sense of guilt. Such guilt feelings are frequently seen in members of religious communities. As I wrote earlier, "For some religious, entering treatment can be guilt-arousing. They may feel constrained to achieve rapid 'cures,' and when these do not occur, they may feel even more guilt because of the cost to the community" (Cerney, 1974, p. 558). Because another is paying the bill, these patients may feel pressured into "getting well," making it difficult to discuss the central issue of how much their life revolves around "pleasing others" — meeting others' expectations.

On the other hand, not paying for one's own treatment can be a way of prolonging treatment. Freud (1913/1958) warned,

> Free treatment enormously increases some of a neurotic's resistances. . . . The absence of the regulating effect offered by the payment of a fee to the doctor makes itself very painfully felt; the whole relationship is removed from the real world, and the patient is deprived of a strong motive for endeavouring to bring the treatment to an end. (p. 132)

What narcissistic gratification it is to have someone listen attentively for a stated period of time, weekly or even oftener! Paying for this time puts the narcissistic gratification in a different perspective.

Just as nonpayment of a fee may be an expression of anger toward the treater, so it can be toward the person(s) who pays for the treatment. It may be a way for the individual to say to the religious community, parents, or spouse, "Now you'll pay, and pay dearly, for all you've done to me" (Cerney, 1974, p. 558). That anger should be addressed directly in treatment and not acted out indirectly. When patients assume responsibility for their portion of the bill, this perception changes in a way that facilitates examination of this issue.

Case Three: Dependency

Free treatment raises the issue of gratitude and indebtedness. "What does the therapist want from me? Sexual favors? Gifts?" I once supervised a resident whose male adolescent patient had been sexually involved with two previous therapists. The patient was hostile and distancing with the resident. The treatment was at a stalemate and the patient was considering dropping out of treatment. Nothing the resident did seemed to make any difference. We worked on the issue of this young man's difficulty trusting another therapist because of his previous experiences. Would this therapist be different? What was the therapist expecting from him? How could the therapist be so nice to him in spite of his obnoxious behavior? Wasn't there something in it for him? Did he expect sexual favors as the other two therapists had?

The resident then talked with the patient about the issue of expecting sexual favors and the guilt that the patient had experienced. He felt that he was receiving something for nothing. (His parents were paying.) This patient was indebted to everyone and felt that he would never get away from the indebtedness!

The therapy then concentrated on issues of dependency—what was being owed and to whom. During the discussion, the patient mentioned his new part-time job that would enable him to buy his own clothes. The therapist suggested that the patient might also consider contributing to his own treatment. On a sliding scale, his fair share would be $2 per session, which would be paid at each session; he would also pay for missed sessions, which had become a problem in recent months. The patient at first responded with considerable resistance, but also showed relief. Exploring this issue brought to light the patient's ambivalence around growing up and assuming adult responsibilities, separating from his parents, and becoming responsible for his own life. Independent adulthood was something this patient both desired and feared.

The patient and therapist agreed on the amount, the manner of payment, and the starting date. Instead of having the bill sent to the parents, the therapist arranged to hand it to the patient, who proudly noted his contributions to the payments. It was his responsibility then to give the bill to his parents. The therapist remarked that the patient appeared to walk a little taller after that. Initiation of the payment plan marked a breakthrough in his treatment. Later, when the patient received a raise, he shyly inquired, "I suppose that means I have to pay three dollars instead of two?" The therapist asked what he thought. The patient smiled as he responded, "It's only fair."

This vignette illustrates how discussion of the fee and its variety of meanings not only facilitated the continuation of therapy, but also highlighted one of the patient's major conflicts: becoming an adult.

Case Four: Guilt Feelings

Not charging a fee or making special accommodations for therapy sessions can engender so much guilt in patients that they may feel that their only alternative is to terminate treatment. Early in my therapeutic work, I agreed to see a young priest at no charge. Initially the treatment went well, but we soon came to a stalemate. I knew we were getting into issues of anger that needed to be addressed, but the patient was unable to discuss them. It struck me that he could not express his obvious irritation with me for bringing up issues he did not want to discuss because I was so nice to see him for free and at his convenience. I asked him if he felt like a charity case. We talked about the special arrangement of fee and time and how he felt that he could not be angry with me (transference or not) because I was doing so much extra for him. He seemed quite relieved when this issue was addressed directly. I asked him if he would feel better if I charged him. His response was "Yes, but I can't afford the standard fee." We looked at his income (which at that time was $300 per month) and agreed that three dollars per session would be an appropriate fee. Once I was being paid, he could address the anger issues quite directly. Gratitude and indebtedness had been getting in the way of his treatment progress.

NONMONETARY PAYMENT

Although charging a fee, even a reduced fee, may be the best solution for dealing with many self-esteem and entitlement issues, it may be difficult to do so with some patients. For example, the federal government pays for treatment of VA patients. Dealing with a sense of entitlement is often a major issue with these patients. However, payment need not always be in money. When it is appropriate in my therapy with VA patients, we agree on an appropriate type of volunteer work. Because the people of the United States are paying for the veteran's treatment, we determine what can be done to repay them. In the hospital, and perhaps even after discharge, the patient may be able to do some volunteer work such as visiting those who are less fortunate. Outside the hospital, we work out some mutually agreeable work such as picking up papers in a park, or some other volunteer work. The time spent in volunteer work is hour for hour of treatment. These patients report a personal investment in their therapy and a sense of reponsibility to help others who are less fortunate—something that continues long after the therapy has ended.

DISCUSSION

Consideration of the role of fees in psychotherapy is not a new topic for discussion. Freud (1913/1958) postulated that the payment of a fee may contribute to the success of a treatment. According to Davids (1964), patients who pay a fee may work harder. Others have argued that fee payment was, like the tip of the iceberg, related to other issues such as resistance, repression, transference, countertransference, and insight (Allen, 1970; Haak, 1957; Koren & Joyce, 1953; Menninger, 1958; Schacht, 1953).

Not all studies, however, support the hypothesis that payment of a fee is beneficial to treatment. Some recent studies suggest it could be detrimental to the process. Mowrer (1963) argued that some patients or clients who pay a fee to a therapist may avoid issues of guilt. Since guilt is so much a motivating factor in why individuals seek treatment, it is difficult to understand how that topic could be avoided in an intensive process with or without the payment of fees.

It would appear that the self-esteem enhancement resulting from paying a reasonable fee would allow for rather than obscure exploration of deeper sources of guilt.

Individuals who are studied in the various fee-no fee studies are difficult to compare because they may differ on a variety of variables, particularly two very important ones: socioeconomic status and diagnosis. Yoken and Berman (1984) attempted to study the fee-no fee issue from the point of patient and therapist. Their clients, graduate students who were offered the opportunity to talk about their problems to a therapist were randomly assigned to a fee-paying ($10) condition or a no-fee control condition. Their therapists (9 advanced students in clinical and counseling psychology) did not know the fee-paying status of the clients they met with in a one-time counseling session. Yoken and Berman concluded that payment of a fee did not enhance treatment. A one-time session with an inexperienced treater is hardly comparable to an in-depth psychotherapy process with an experienced treater.

Manos (1982) reported a more extended study with therapy ranging from 4 to 14 months. Eight second-year residents were the therapists of these 28 patients (15 college or university students, 8 employees, 2 technicians, and 3 housewives). The therapists concluded that nonpayment of a fee had no influence on treatment in 65% (18) cases and some negative influence in about 35% (10) cases. Although the length of therapy was more acceptable in this study, inexperienced treaters may not detect the subtleties of the meaning of below-cost or no-fee treatment. As I mentioned earlier, my didactic and supervisory experience, along with that of my colleagues, suggests that it is the rare second-year resident who can appreciate or detect the impact of fee upon treatment. Aware of their inexperience, they are too conflicted about charging any fee. One resident remarked, "We should pay the patients for allowing us to practice on them" — a comment reflective of the feeling of many inexperienced residents.

Raney (1982-1983) looked at detailed clinical examples in the literature. He found that the issue of fee, when not directly discussed and resolved, made its appearance in metaphors and lack of movement in the therapy. The patient's behavior as seen in the clinical content could be interpreted as an attempt to rectify complications around the fee particularly when the patient felt it was too low and not in accord with one's ability to pay. Paris (1982-1983) observed a tendency for treatment to break up or prematurely terminate when the issue of fee was not worked through. Their work and analyses closely parallel my clinical experience and that of my colleagues.

In the United States, paying one's way is a mark of status and enhances self-esteem. We expect to pay for psychotherapy. This does not mean that psychotherapy cannot begin on a free basis or with someone else — insurance or parents — paying for it. One of the most critical turning points in psychotherapy can be the discussion around one's dependence upon others and one's efforts to be financially independent. One external manifestation of this beginning movement is frequently seen in beginning to pay for one's own treatment — gradually at first until it is possible to assume the responsibility entirely.

The fee a patient pays for therapy is much more than a specified amount of money. It encompasses an entire repertoire of meanings for both patient and therapist. Krueger (1986b) wrote:

> Americans have been raised in a culture with informal ethical and social strictures concerning the impropriety of candid discussion of money, fees, and personal income. In addition, individual meanings and attributions hitchhike on the issue of money and further complicate our money-associated behaviors. (p. vii)

Treatments are interrupted (Paris, 1982-1983) or only superficially completed by avoiding the discussion of money and all its many meanings for a particular patient.

By listening to patients, therapists can detect metaphors directly connected with patients' feelings about money, their fee, and our position in regard to these issues. More frequently than not, however, we choose another aspect to interpret, and bypass the money issue, despite the admonitions of outstanding clinicians from Freud to Krueger.

Behavior pertaining to the fee and to paying the bill can be a metaphor for ambivalence about becoming a responsible adult. It can highlight feelings of inferiority and second-class citizenship, and it can adversely affect the patient's fledgling self-esteem. It can hide fears of progress and fears of examining anticipated frightening revelations in an effort to maintain the status quo. Different cultures, ethnic groups, social structures, and each individual within these groups imbue money with many conscious and unconscious equations. Family values, developmental issues, and emotional needs all influence how an individual will look at the issue of money. Such an important issue must not be ignored in therapy, but particularly in therapies that must make an adjustment in fee. The purpose of psychotherapy is not to confirm feelings of second-class citizenship, but to enhance the realization that we are each precious, unique, and of inestimable worth.

REFERENCES

Allen, A. (1970). The fee as a therapeutic tool. *Psychoanalytic Quarterly*, *40*, 132-140.

Cerney, M.S. (1974). Psychiatric services for religious. *Sisters Today*, *45*, 556-561.

Davids, A. (1964). The relation of cognitive-dissonance theory to an aspect of psychotherapeutic practice. *American Psychologist*, *19*, 329-332.

Freud, S. (1958). On beginning the treatment. In J. Strachey (Ed. and Trans.), *The standard edition of the complete psychological works of Sigmund Freud* (Vol. 12, pp. 121-144). London: Hogarth Press. (Original work published 1913).

Haak, N. (1957). Comments on the analytic situation. *International Journal of Psychoanalysis*, *38*, 183-195.

In re H. Jon Geis, P.C. v. Landau, 458 N.Y.S. 2d 1000 (N.Y. City Ct. 1983).

Koren, L., & Joyce, J. (1953). The treatment implications of payment of fees in a clinic setting. *American Journal of Orthopsychiatry*, *23*, 350-357.

Krueger, D.W. (1986a). Money, success, and success phobia. In D.W. Krueger (Ed.), *The last taboo* (pp. 3-15). New York: Brunner/Mazel.

Krueger, D.W. (1986b). Preface. In D.W. Krueger (Ed.), *The last taboo* (pp. vii-ix). New York: Brunner/Mazel.

Manos, N. (1982). Free psychotherapy: The therapist's and the patient's view. *Psychotherapy and Psychosomatics*, *37*, 137-143.

Menninger, K. (1958). *Theory of psychoanalytic technique*. New York: Basic Books.

Paris, J. (1982-1983). Frame disturbances in no-fee psychotherapy. *International Journal of Psychoanalytic Psychotherapy*, *9*, 135-146.

Raney, J. (1982-1983). The payment of fees for psychotherapy. *International Journal of Psychoanalytic Psychotherapy, 9,* 147-181.

Schacht, M. (1953). The technique of employing doctor-patient transactions in psychoanalysis. *American Journal of Psychotherapy, 7,* 653-663.

Yoken, C. & Berman, J. (1984). Does paying a fee for psychotherapy alter the effectiveness of treatment? *Journal of Consulting and Clinical Psychology, 52*(2), 254-260.

Clouded Horizons:
One Perspective of Poverty

Karen Simpson Callaway

SUMMARY. A framework constructed from elements of Bronfen-brenner's ecology of human development theory and a social learning approach to object-relations theory is proposed to provide a systematic way of exploring the experiential world of the lower socioeconomic status psychotherapy patient. Following this framework, the association between victimization and powerlessness is explored in relation to conceptions of reality that are often held by lower status individuals, which tends to constrict their available life choices.

Regardless of the psychotherapy model, to understand the phenomenal world of the patient is usually seen as critical in order to help the patient gain personal insight or to cope more effectively with his or her world. For the middle-to-upper-class therapist, understanding the world and perspective of the lower class patient may not come easily or naturally. Combining terminology from object-relations theory and Urie Bronfenbrenner's (1977) ecology of human development theory provides a schema which can guide us in gathering information about the experiences of the poor.

Understanding the development of disorders and knowing what to do about them often requires going beyond the immediate interpersonal behaviors of one or two persons in one place; it demands the examination of multiperson systems of interaction in multiple settings while taking into account aspects of the environment that

Karen Simpson Callaway received her master's degree in psychology from San Diego State University, and is currently working toward a PhD in clinical psychology at the University of Utah. Mailing address: Department of Psychology, Salt Lake City, UT 84112.

67

are beyond the subject's immediate situation. We must uncover the system of people, events, and ideas which have influenced the subject's life.

These influential people, events, and ideas set the context for what the individual adapts to and for what is learned about the world and about the self. These are the "objects" of object-relationsr theory. An object can be defined as a person, place, thing, idea, fantasy, or memory invested with emotional energy (love or hate or more modulated combinations of love and hate). An external object is a person, place, or thing invested with emotional energy. An internal object is an idea, fantasy, or memory pertaining to a person, place, or thing (Hamilton, 1988, p. 7). Interactions with objects can be internalized by introjection, a process initially described by Harry Stack Sullivan (1953), where the individual learns to treat himself or herself as important others (or other important objects) have treated him or her in the past. Introjection connects the social milieu with the intrapsychic functioning of the individual.

The ecological system perspective of Bronfenbrenner (1977) provides a useful framework for reminding us of the interpersonal, social, and cultural objects or influences which affect the poor. He divides the ecological environment into four nested systems, each contained within the next.

At the simplest level is the microsystem, which can be defined as the relationships between the person and the environment in a setting with particular physical features, activities, roles, and times. The setting could be the home, the workplace, a school, or any another setting that the individual engages with regularly. This level has been the traditional focus of object-relations and interpersonal theories that have examined the relationship between the patient and significant others and the patient's introjections of past relationships. The microsystems of the poor are likely to be experientially divergent from the microsystems of the middle and upper classes. For instance, children growing up in a lower socioeconomic status (SES) family are more likely to have alcoholic parents, parents with psychological disorders (Dohrenwend & Dohrenwend, 1981), parents who are unemployed or poorly educated; and they are more likely to be raised in a more authoritarian manner with physical punishments (Kohn, 1972). As a result, a neglectful attitude toward the self may be introjected from the neglectful actions of parents with impaired functioning. Physical punishments can be internalized as a punishing self. Introjects reflect the internalization of the ways the parents have treated the child.

For many lower SES individuals the workplace is a dehumanizing and routine experience where they have little control over working conditions. The woman who works for a non-union factory, is treated as a replaceable unit, where she and her interests and needs are neglected, may internalize this message as neglect of her own potential. If others do not see her as important, it is less likely that she will view herself as important.

Influential objects at the microsystem level have direct impacts on the individual, but at the next level of the mesosystem the effects are less direct. The mesosystem is a system made up of the relationships between the major settings containing the person at a particular point in his or her life; it is a system of microsystems. For a child this level might include interactions among the family, school, and peer group. Examples of mesosystems which impact children living in poverty could consist of having fewer family interactions with the school system than higher SES families, or a poor child's friends dropping out of school, creating a family and peer group conflict. The nature of an individual's interactions within microsystems is partially dependent on the nature of the interactions between microsystems. Tensions between family and school can function to set the tone for the child's home and classroom interactions.

The third level, the exosystem, includes formal and informal social structures that do not contain the person directly but impinge upon or encompass the immediate settings in which that person is found, and influences what occurs there. Included are the major institutions of society as they operate on a concrete local level. The neighborhood, agencies of government, the distribution of goods and services, communication and transportation facilities, and the mass media are examples used by Bronfenbrenner to illustrate the exosystem. Living in a neighborhood which is dangerous, chaotic, powerless, and without norms probably results in a view of the world that is quite discrepant from that of those who live in neighborhoods which are supportive, organized, normed, and influential. Having to interact with the often less-than-friendly employment office, welfare office, or county hospital would have dramatically different results in the view one takes of reality than having to interact with the accountant's office, the savings and loan, or the private family physician. Being treated as unimportant, in conjunction with not being able to adequately get one's needs met from institutions, can also be internalized as a neglectful attitude toward oneself.

The fourth and most abstract level is the macrosystem. This system includes the overarching institutional patterns of the culture or subculture, and refers to the general prototypes that set the pattern for the structures and activities that occur on a concrete level. Most macrosystems are informal and implicit, making up the ideology which unfolds as custom and practice in everyday life that gives meaning and motivation to particular agencies, roles, activities and their interrelations. Cultural values set the context for how our society and institutions view the poor. One aspect of our macrosystem is the value we place on the work ethic. The work ethic of our culture means one thing to those who have steady, reliable employment and another thing to those who are unemployed with no foreseeable job prospects. Pressure resulting from the cultural value of being self-supporting can result in feeling blamed for being unemployed and feeling inferior to those with job opportunities, creating the possibility for the internalization of self-doubt and self-blame.

Other macrosystem aspects include our cultural adoration of material goods and our tendencies toward defining ourselves by our occupations. These ideologies are unremittingly reflected in television programming, serving to highlight the feelings of deprivation and lack of self-worth of those in poverty who aspire to similar lifestyles. Lacking the opportunities or the knowledge of how to achieve their aspirations, the poor may develop a feeling of being blocked and restricted by their social position. The internalization of being blocked and restricted as a result of unobtainable social values could manifest itself as a holding back of one's self, of blocking the self from growing.

Each of the higher levels affect the lower systems in a hierarchical pattern. The individual growing up in a low SES family is not only affected by his or her family, school, and peer interactions, but indirectly through the exosystem's influence on the microsystems. The dehumanizing nature of becoming a case number to a bureaucratic social service agency affects the parent's view of herself and she in turn affects her children.

Attitudes toward the poor are shaped by our economic ideology and cultural norms; these attitudes shape the nature of social policies, social service agencies, schools, and neighborhoods. Many seem to believe that survival of the fittest implies that those of the lower classes have fewer abilities and are less able to succeed because of some natural selection procedure. This kind of attitude functions to blame the victim, and to discount their needs for more and better education, childcare, and employment opportunities.

These four interconnected system levels all have an interacting part in shaping the strategies we learn for relating to others, for achieving goals, and for coping with stress. They contain the objects that are emotionally meaningful to us that we adapt to and learn from on a day-to-day basis. As individuals, we internalize repeated interactions, not only with others who are close to us, but interactions with our neighborhoods and institutions that affect our daily lives. The nature of the interactions between microsystems affects the way we operate within them and the overriding values of our culture structure the way in which the micro- and exosystems operate. It is within this elaborate system that self-concepts are formed and ways of adapting to the social environment are learned. Using Bronfenbrenner's ecological system as a way of orienting ourselves to a multileveled complex structure permits us to systematically view social interactions on a larger canvas, and to avoid reductionistic conceptions of the lower class patient.

Maladaptive or pathological personality patterns occur when alternative strategies are few in number and are practiced rigidly, when the person's habitual perceptions, needs, and behaviors perpetuate and intensify preexisting difficulties; and when there is a lack of resilience under conditions of subjective stress (Millon, 1981). John Mirowsky (1986) demonstrates how macrosystem and exosystem variables can impact the alternative strategies of the lower SES person by arguing that maladaptive patterns and strategies arise from beliefs and concerns that reflect the nature of the social world. The social world of the poor is characterized by powerlessness and by the threat of victimization and exploitation. Mirowsky points out that whenever resources and opportunities are scarce, wherever exploitation and victimization are common, and wherever the protection provided by institutions and agencies is weak, mistrust is a reasonable orientation toward others. The beliefs and concerns that give rise to the maladaptive patterns are learned from the social environment, as are the intrapsychic internalizations of neglecting one's potential, holding back the self, or self-doubt that can develop from having needs repeatedly ignored by bureaucratic institutions, by being blocked by lack of education, and by feeling inferior to the models of upward mobility that are portrayed on television.

In the United States, studies indicate that lower SES individuals are more likely to be victims of assault, robbery, purse snatching, pocket-picking, personal larceny, rape, and attempted rape (Parsisi, Gottfredson, Hindelang, & Flanagan, 1979). They also live in an environment where they are often subjected to unpredictable exploitation. The poor are more likely to worry about being burglarized, being raped, or being cheated by corporations (Parsisi et al., 1979). This is the nature of the exosystem that lower SES individuals must learn from and adapt to.

Mirowsky and Ross (1983) found the experience of powerlessness to be related to beliefs of external control: that important outcomes are due to luck, fate, or powerful others, more than by one's own preference, choice, or action. This belief in external control combined with the fear of victimization and exploitation results in a characteristic mistrust of others, and a belief that one person's position can only be improved at the expense of another's. Kohn's (1972) research supports this position, finding that the lower socioeconomic classes seem to value conformity to external authority; they have rigid, conservative views of man and social institutions, fearfulness and distrust, and a fatalistic belief that one is at the mercy of forces and people beyond one's control and often beyond one's understanding. When faced with a chaotic and menacing environment that appears uncontrollable, it is not difficult to imagine how these attitudes become adaptive in ongoing interactions with a threatening neighborhood, a dehumanizing workplace or welfare office. The threats of victimization and exploitation are themes often expressed by lower status mental patients. The lower class patients feel exploited, believe that society is organized against them, and have a deep mistrust of its institutional representatives (Mirowsky, 1986). Lower class patients are more likely to express "paranoid" beliefs.

Rotter (1980) found that individuals who assume that others cannot be trusted are less aware of information that would help them judge trustworthiness, creating a cycle supportive of mistrust. While it may be adaptive in some social environments to be suspicious or mistrustful, inflexibly applying such a strategy can decrease the awareness of information which could help a suspicious individual find supportive, trustworthy people and situations. Kohn (1972) points out that not only does this conception of reality make it harder to judge trustworthiness, but

> There are times when a defensive posture invites attack, and there are times when the assumption that one is at the mercy of forces beyond one's control — even though they are justified — leaves one all the more at their mercy. (p. 301)

The habitual perception of mistrust perpetuates the preexisting difficulty of powerlessness, beliefs in external control, and vulnerability to further exploitation and victimization, creating a maladaptive behavior pattern. From Mirowsky's and Kohn's arguments, identifying macrosystem ideologies such as the unequal distribution of resources, and exosystem variables such as unsafe neighborhoods and lack of protection have a place in understanding the maladaptive personality development of the low SES patient.

It becomes apparent that the conditions of life vary dramatically in the hierarchy of social class, and that subjective reality is necessarily different across classes. The conditions of life for the poor allow little freedom of action; there are few reasons to feel in control of fate. Kohn (1972) states:

> To be lower class is to be insufficiently educated, to work at a job of little substantive complexity, under conditions of close supervision, and with little leeway to vary a routine flow of work. These are precisely the conditions that narrow one's conception of reality and reduce one's sense of personal efficacy. (p. 301)

As conceptions of reality become narrower, and as self-worth becomes threatened, life choices diminish, options become fewer, and doors close. One becomes blocked, with the only apparent option being apathetic compliance. The experience of powerlessness, of having no economic power, little social influence, and none of the power that knowledge brings, can radically obscure the visible horizon of possibilities.

The lower SES person does tend to be more affected by people and events outside his or her control. These people have less control over jobs, neighborhoods, homes, and life-styles than those with middle class status. Hess (1970) suggests that a common adaptive reaction to the social situation of powerlessness is to adopt attitudes of low self-esteem, dependency, and passivity. Children of such parents will learn to be apathetic and relatively helpless when they encounter stress in later life, thus reducing their resiliency under conditions of subjective stress. They will not have acquired the necessary flexibility of adaptive responses that their middle-class peers will have acquired. Perceptions and strategies which are based on conformity to authority oversimplify the social reality, and this fearful view does not permit taking advantage of options that might otherwise be open (Kohn, 1972). Using passivity and apathy as a way of coping with powerlessness only serves to ultimately reduce the number of ways out of poverty, to further advance the fog on the horizon, to limit the number of alternative strategies.

The lower class conception of reality (e.g., beliefs in external control, in a hostile world requiring distrust, and conformity to authority) is shaped by actual conditions and may often be useful. When risks of victimization are higher, keeping one's guard up serves a useful function. However, when the habitual perceptions and behaviors such as distrust, external control, and conformity perpetuate and intensify preexisting difficulties, when the number of alternative strategies are reduced, and when a vulnerability to stress emerges, the conception of reality becomes a maladaptive pattern which functions to severely limit the available choices of the lower SES patient. Choices become even more limited and vulnerabilities greater when intrapsychic internalizations of neglecting one's potential, holding back the self, and self-doubt are present. Their horizons become clouded, and their lives constrained.

An individual's personality patterns, perceptions, and associated behaviors may have many determinants: genetics, biochemistry, learning, expectations, situational variables, social and cultural variables, and a certain amount of random variance (Benjamin, 1988). In order to begin to understand those determinants so that strategic interventions can be made, we can examine the patient's world as the patient experiences it. Keeping in mind the microsystem, mesosystem, exosystem, and macrosystem levels can help the therapist to more fully reconstruct the influential experiences that shape the world of lower SES patients.

REFERENCES

Benjamin, L. S. (1988). *SASB short form users manual.* Salt Lake City, UT: INTREX Interpersonal Institute.

Benjamin, L. S. (1986). Adding social and intrapsychic descriptors of Axis I of DSMIII. In T. Millon & G. L. Klerman (Eds.), *Contemporary directions in psychopathology.* New York: Guilford Press.

Bronfenbrenner, U. (1977). Toward an experimental ecology of human development. *American Psychologist, 32,* 513-530.

Dohrenwend, B. P., & Dohrenwend, B. S. (1981). Socioenvironmental factors, stress, and psychopathology. *American Journal of Community Psychology, 9,* 128-159.

Hess, R. D. (1970). The transmission of cognitive strategies in poor families: The socialization of apathy and underachievement. In V. L. Allen (Ed.), *Psychological factors in poverty* (pp. 72-92). Chicago: Markham Press.

Kohn, M. L. (1972). Class, family and schizophrenia: A reformulation. *Social Forces, 50,* 295-304.

Hamilton, N. G. (1988). *Self and others: Object relations theory in practice.* Northvale, NJ: Jason Aronson.

Millon, T. (1981). *Disorders of personality: DSM-III: Axis II.* New York: John Wiley & Sons.

Mirowsky, J. (1986). Disorder and its context: Paranoid beliefs of thought problems, hallucinations, and delusions under threatening social conditions. *Research in Community and Mental Health, 5,* 185-204.

Mirowsky, J., & Ross, C. E. (1983). Paranoia and the structure of powerlessness. *American Sociological Review, 48,* 228-239.

Parisi, N., Gottfredson, M. R., Hindelang, M. J., & Flanagan, T. J. (1979). *Sourcebook on criminal justice statistics-1978.* Washington, DC: U.S. Government Printing Office.

Rotter, J.B. (1980). Interpersonal trust, trustworthiness, and gullibility. *American Psychologist, 35,* 1-7.

Sullivan, H. S. (1953). *The Interpersonal Theory of Psychiatry.* Washington, DC: The William Alanson White Psychiatric Foundation.

Pro-Choice

Emily Simerly

SUMMARY. Life is made up of core courses and electives. In the College of Hard Knocks, psychotherapy is an elective. Those of us who profess to deliver this service struggle in varying degrees with the issue of fees and charges and what to do about prospective clients who cannot pay. This article addresses that nagging problem with a retro, '60s idealism coupled with some pragmatic, '90s, kinder, gentler suggestions.

Life is made up of core courses and electives. In the College of Hard Knocks, psychotherapy is an elective. It is not unusual for the poor to take what they can get and make the best of it. Our jobs as psychotherapists are to reduce the elitism in our field and provide alternatives and choices. This is not easy; often the price of consciousness is the relinquishment of privilege. This article addresses the dilemma of this need for psychotherapy and the delivery of those services in a creative but nonsacrificial way.

Over time, and probably not on purpose, we have colluded as a profession to exclude poor people from our midst. For instance, in Atlanta, most psychotherapists are located on the north and east sides of the city, which are not where the majority of poor people live. The professionals I know rarely worry about being on a public transportation line, which is a must for working with low socioeconomic groups. This placement of therapists in a geographically distant location from the poor is financially logical because clients are pulled primarily from the north and east sides. Unfortunately, it

Emily Simerly is a doctoral student in clinical psychology in the specialty track area of psychotherapy at Georgia State University in Atlanta, GA. Current mailing address: 1005 Tenth Avenue, Albany, GA 31701.

also limits the options for people who are poor, who need treatment, and who depend on public transportation.

It is no secret that we are an expensive group, so that poor people usually don't show up at our door. And at the common rate of $90 per session, there are a lot more "poor" people in our consumer group than before. Therapy for the most part is a verbal endeavor, and we often assume or believe that poor people don't really have the "necessary verbal skills." Insight is not viewed as a particular need or forte of theirs because they lead (or so we think) a "simpler" life. They don't seem to have the "angst" of the intellectual. This is most likely because that angst gets buried under the hierarchy of needs where survival is primary.

To make matters worse, therapists add the idea that "if you really wanted to be in therapy, you would find the money." While that may often be the case in our familiar circles of clients, it is for the poor a subtle way of blaming the victim. This is coupled with the naively vulgar consideration that if a client gets therapy for free, the therapy will not be valued. We therapists would be wiser to realize there may be an interaction of this dictum with the ability to pay. Those who cannot afford to pay may very well get something out of free or nearly free therapy. This is true for the chronically poor as well as for chronically ill patients, like Persons With Aids (PWAs), who are in places where they need the most therapy of their lives and often have the fewest resources.

Additionally, there exists among our ranks some lack of appreciation for county mental health centers, the very places that welcome the poor. This double-binds the poor: They can't pay and yet what they can get isn't really good enough. This reminds me of pro-life forces who believe that adoption and not abortion is the answer. The only problem is that those same forces aren't willing or interested in adopting the babies, mostly minorities, who are available. Similarly, we therapists often aren't willing to sacrifice for poor clients, but we disparage the help they can get.

Finally, with the American Psychological Association's most current Ethical Procedures (1981), dual relationships are no longer considered ethical. A number of my graduate student colleagues and other financially strapped folks have often used bartering of services as a means to be in therapy. While the ethics code is ultimately for the good of the client, it still serves to limit choices and means to achieve ends.

We are at least cognitively aware of the problems of the poor. An example is the deal we (society) offer to make with young poor girls. We let them know that if they get pregnant out of wedlock, and if they do not marry the father, and if they do not have any income, then we reward them with a guaranteed income and a free apartment. If, on the other hand, they do marry or openly live with the father, they are punished by these rewards being removed. This is, of course, no choice at all. In their place, I also would have little problem choosing between the alternatives.

I worked for a while at a huge public hospital in Atlanta. One day, when passing through the lobby waiting room that virtually teems with the poor and wretched, I noticed an elderly heavy-set man dressed in overalls. On his massive knee rested a large, black, supple Bible, frayed at the edges. I was very touched by the picture of this old man, waiting patiently and resting his hand on what I now think of as the ultimate transitional object.

During the same interim, I was seeing a client at another location for psychotherapy. This client lived in an upper-middle-class area of town. On the same day that I saw the old man, this client came in complaining that his parents were not providing the support adequate to maintain the life-style to which he would like to become accustomed. He would have to exercise at home instead of at an exercise gym; he would have to spend only 2 weeks at the beach that summer instead of the full month he had anticipated. I am not (at this point in my life) a religious type, but I had a strong urge to put a Bible on his knee, just to see what would happen. I didn't do that and instead struggled with the seeming banality of his problems. I was able to get beyond that relative banality to the absolute person, but I never forgot the paradox of the seemingly peaceful poor old man and the tormented wealthy young man. Their similarity, and what was so hard for the young man, was a lack of alternatives.

George Lamming (1983) speaks to a "fractured consciousness" that in his Caribbean world meant the "psychological injury inflicted by the sacred rule that all forms of social status would be determined by the degrees of skin complexion" (p. xi). Skin complexion is not the only mediator of social class in our world anymore. Decidedly, the percentages go to blacks and other minorities, but in the South I live in, there are whites who are as poor and scorned. Frantz Fanon (1968) noted that blacks are not only black, they are black in relation to whites. Similarly, poor are not just poor, they are poor in relation to all other groups.

Reverend Ike was once quoted in the *Village Voice* as saying "The best thing you can do for poor people is not be one of them." He took this to heart, as have many evangelists, but there is a danger in his belief. A cautionary note is warranted here or we may add this to our repertoire of skills of excluding poor people. That is, we won't sacrifice any income because that wouldn't be the "best thing" for poor people. It is easy and seductive to believe poor people will only respect us if we have fortunes and show it.

I used to be afflicted with what I call Liberals' Disease. It generally attacks the middle and upper classes, with symptoms like setting "softer" limits on poor people and bending the rules because their lives have been so bad. Even when I realized that it really was the most insipid form of patronizing, I found it quite difficult to quit. Elizabeth Janeway (1980) spoke to this in a similar way, noting that those in power tend to justify paternal actions by saying the motives of such actions are benevolent and in the best interests of the recipient, and also that the ones who are being helped don't actually know what they want and probably couldn't help themselves if they knew.

The answer to this problem is not to patronize but to offer a legitimate choice, in whatever way we can. I used to do therapy with poor people out of my Sucker Parent. I "kindly" felt they deserved a break. If they didn't pay, I tended to overlook it for a long time. I knew I was still in control, and that I would just let it ride while they worked it out. I was doing it for their "own good." In other words, I was making their choice for them, not giving them one. Heller (1985) notes that the real power for clients to gain is to be able to stand in the face of life's uncertainty. While parts of life are uncertain for us all, the day-to-day uncertainty of the poor must be very hard to bear. Let's not kid ourselves that patronizing is actually any form of strength-building of our clients.

As a student, I can relate to the day-in and day-out struggle of making ends meet. Eric Berne failed to discuss the Financial Ego State, which is far more powerful than the other three. When I have a bad month and am not able to meet bill payments, I feel tremendous anxiety that bleeds into the rest of my life. I find myself choosing to do what often is unhealthy for me, like taking on more work than I should. I assume this is the case for the poor.

I am a child of the '60s and I still carry those ideals deep within me. I have tried to contain my Liberals' Disease, but I know I still carry seeds of prejudice. I also know my job is not to feed those seeds. Clearing out the Liberals' Disease allows for a cleaner need I have for justice and equality for all. Now all that is left is the responsibility, and particularly, how to respond with a cost/benefit analysis so that everybody wins. Virginia Woolf (1929) described a time in her life when she suddenly received a surprise inheritance annually for life from an aunt. This came at about the same time that women got the right to vote. She felt the money was infinitely more important. The money rid her of her fear and bitterness and opened for her, as she said, "a view of the open sky" (p. 39). It was clear to her "what a change of temper a fixed income will bring about."

In the end, we all make our own choices. Unfortuntately for poor people, when we try to decide how to "help" them, our dilemmas are often solved at their expense. Rationalization is an easy task when it's saving us money. The idea of charity has seemed always to be offensive to poor people. What I'd like to see in the place of charity is creativity in the direction of treatment options for the poor. Some thoughts include a possibility such as Psychotherapy Aid, like Legal Aid, that provides therapy for those not able to afford it. Assigning, say, 3 hours per week for virtually free therapy ($5.00-$10.00) is an option. Offering free supervision to mental health workers, or consultation to their supervisors, or offering group psychotherapy at a public psychiatric ward are other alternatives that could meet an idealistic need in a practical way that is still not too taxing to the provider.

I'm all for making money. This psychotherapy path I chose was my path with heart, but knowing it could provide me a good living didn't hurt. In fact, I would not have chosen it if it had not. But as of this writing I intend to live my professional life in a way that gives back some of what I've received and that somehow adds to the balance of existence. This may be too little in the long run, but when I think that way, I remember the little sparrow lying on its back with its feet up in the air. A rider came along and asked what it was doing. The sparrow said, "I heard the sky is falling and I'm going to hold it up." The rider was derisive and said "You can't hold the sky up with your scrawny legs!" "One does what one can," said the sparrow, "one does what one can."

Poor people are economic prey. Notice the prices at grocery stores in ghettos. That is because of an absence of choices. The poor often can't hop into a car and drive to another store for cheaper prices. Thus, there are practical issues that seasoned therapists know. Poor people often don't show up for appointments, for transportation or other reasons. Their realities are different. They missed the bus. Their ride didn't come. They couldn't get off from work. They got a chance to work overtime at the last minute and weren't able to call. We need to protect ourselves from these variables as much as we do with our other clients, even while remembering that poor people have different contingencies from most of us.

Tracy Chapman is a singer who has recently taken the world by storm. One of her songs speaks to her vision of poor people finally taking up the banner and revolting against their lot. As I said, I am a child of the '60s and I still have those ideals. But given the sad state of the liberal (so-called) coalition these days, I don't see happening what I wish Ms. Chapman was right about. I don't see people rising up. Instead, I see poor kids hoping and dreaming of becoming a rock star or a football player. Failing that, turning to crime is a far easier and probably more successful route than the long road up to the middle class. Shunned and without resources, the poor not only know their place, they are stuck in it. Accessibility is only a distant and hard-fought-for part of their lives.

In the end, offering alternatives to poor people in the way of whatever services we can give can only add to the possibility of emancipation from the chains of poverty. We can release our need for them to benefit from our provisions and instead simply make a space available to them. They will have a choice about becoming psychotherapy clients. And if we do our work well, those who are poor can become empowered and, through empowerment, add to the richness of their lives. *This* choice is ours.

REFERENCES

American Psychological Association. (1981). Ethical principles of Psychologists. *American Psychologist, 36*(6), 633-638.

Fanon, F. (1967). *Black skin, white masks.* New York: Grove Press.

Heller, D. (1985). *Power in psychotherapeutic practice.* New York: Human Sciences Press.

Janeway, E. (1980). *Powers of the weak.* New York: Alfred Knopf.

Lamming, G. (1983). *In the castle of my skin.* New York: Schocken Books.

Woolf, V. (1929). *A room of one's own.* New York: Harcourt, Brace, & Jovanovich.

Transference and Countertransference in Cross-Cultural Therapies

Hanneke Bot

SUMMARY. A brief overview of sociocultural influences in Kenya is followed by discussion of the treatment of an African Kenyan male patient by a white expatriate female therapist, with focus on transference and countertransference aspects involved in cross-cultural therapy. Problems created by racial differences and the feelings of both parties are mutually experienced obstacles to the therapy, but can be of tremendous value to both patient and therapist.

This paper is based on my experiences as a psychotherapist working mainly with low- and middle-class patients in Nairobi, Kenya. As I am expatriate, and white, racial tensions are part and parcel of the therapies I conduct with Kenyan clients. All the prejudices that go with racial differences, together with the intensity of feelings of frustration and anger on one side and guilt on the other, add an extra dimension to the encounters; but if acknowledged and dealt with as mutually experienced obstacles, they can be of tremendous value to both the patient and the therapist.

First I will give a short impression of the sociocultural background of my clients and then will describe how this influences the development of transference and countertransference, illustrating these mechanisms with a case description. An important factor turns out to be the racial and colonial history that I share with my patients, although each from our own stance.

Hanneke Bot, MSc, Sociology, worked as a psychotherapist in Nairobi, Kenya. Now back in the Netherlands, she is engaged in the private practice of psychotherapy. Mailing address: Balkerveste 7, 3432 AB Nieuwegein, Netherlands.

SOCIOCULTURAL INFLUENCES

Kenya is far from a psychologically oriented society. While individuation is a process that goes together with "development" and "modernization," it is a developing characteristic of Kenyan society; however, strong adherence to group norms still dominates. Most of my adult clients grew up in extended-family situations, learning from an early age to cope with a large number of people around them, but in an atmosphere where expression of personal feelings is definitely not encouraged (Nelson, 1987).

The educational system, at home and in school, is characterized by emphasis on discipline, obedience, and rote learning. Elders, friends, and relatives are consulted for advice on social and psychological problems. Yet increasing reliance on pharmacological palliatives is evident. Medical doctors, including psychiatrists, are so heavily overloaded that they devote only a few minutes to patients and rely on medication.

People who have grown up in such a setting usually find it odd to have to talk, to express their feelings, and to assume initiative in treatment as is customary in psychotherapy. Although most often they come for therapy after they have discovered that traditional methods or medication did not help them sufficiently, it takes quite some time and reorientation for them to adjust to the prevailing model of psychological treatment.

Race relations in Kenya are a sensitive issue. Although officially the various races coexist peacefully, the reality is different. Generally speaking, there are three groups: black African Kenyans, white and Asian Kenyans, and expatriates (mainly Whites and Asian Kenyans, resident in the country who do not hold citizenship). The attitude toward Whites, whether citizens or expatriates, is ambivalent. On one hand they are seen as strong, knowledgeable, and superior. On the other hand, their motives are suspect: "They will try to conquer us again, they do not understand us, they look down upon us"—all tinged with jealousy, resentment, and anger.

These factors influence the therapeutic relationship. And one can see that the socially conditioned dependence on advice increases submissive attitudes in the transference: "You will tell me what I have to do." On the other hand, everything you say that does not suit them can easily be dismissed: "We Africans see such things differently."

TRANSFERENCE

In my experience, most clients greatly appreciate the opportunity to talk and to be listened to. But as soon as I try to help them express any feelings toward me, they usually fall silent, or say something like "But you are the doctor." The idea that one even dares to entertain "feelings" toward a doctor is entirely new.

At the same time, I find that addressing the transference is vital for the therapy and that especially the race relationship has to be talked about very early. Whenever I see a possibility to address the issue, I will do it.

One of my clients said during the first interview: "My father used to work for a mzungu [white man] and got very little pay." I replied, "And here you sit with another mzungu, from the same category as the one who exploited your father. How does that feel?" Although he said that this was entirely different, my comment established for him that the topic was not taboo, and in later sessions we were able to talk about it again.

A colleague pointed out to me what he called the "built-in transference" that some clients have: "They accept you because you are there to help them, even though—or maybe because—you are white" (C. Peltzer, personal communication, 1986). He suggested using it, developing it to build up a transference relationship faster. While I think he is right in valuing these positive transference feelings, and his remarks made me appreciate them better, I have found that they can also serve to disguise negative feelings as the therapy proceeds.

COUNTERTRANSFERENCE

Countertransference has received particular attention in cross-cultural therapies, for it is supposed that cultural differences between client and therapist can seriously harm the treatment, usually in the context of countertransference feelings. I used to think shared knowledge about the other culture would be of great help to solve the problem. But I have found that more is involved than lack of information. Cross-cultural differences are usually not just "cultural": They are economic, social, political, racial, colonial; they are often unconscious or manifest in vague feelings of estrangement. Although knowledge of the sociocultural history of both patient and therapist is an important tool for acknowledging and understanding countertransference feelings, it is not sufficient to deal with the strong feelings that can be induced in cross-everything therapies.

Gorkin (1986; Gorkin, Massalha, & Yetziv, 1985) a Jewish-American clinician who treats Arab clients in Israel, describes several of these countertransference phenomena very clearly. He speaks of the therapist's frequent curiosity about the patient's views in respect to many areas; the guilt about the unequal economic positions, the colonial culture, aggression embedded in the therapist's "superior" status, the tendency to present oneself as different from other white colonialists. And all this had to be confronted.

Because it is often so interesting and seems so important when the client talks about these issues, it is sometimes difficult to distinguish between "interesting" and "therapeutic," and one sometimes feels tempted to ask questions just to satisfy one's own curiosity. The client I will describe later in this paper was very interested in African literature and had definite ideas about colonialism. While I was treating him, Wole Soyinka received the Nobel Award for Literature. I wondered how my patient felt about it: Did he see Soyinka as a traitor, accepting a prize from the white establishment, or was he proud that an African was finally awarded such an important distinction? He did not mention the issue. And I did not ask him.

One experiences the alienating feeling of empathizing with the anger of the client — anger against Whites, colonialism, and exploitation — while at the same time it is also directed at you. This may lead to the therapist trying to show that he or she is different from those "other Whites" and trying to hide some of the features of his or her own comfortable life from the patient.

JOHN

Although I recognize the above elements in various degrees in treatment of most of my African clients, I will discuss here one particular patient, John, who has helped me to understand these phenomena. He exhibited his transference feelings in such an outspoken manner that I could hardly restrain myself, and experienced equally strong countertransference feelings. Ordinarily I feel that African Kenyans develop a transference relationship very slowly, John was an absolute exception to this rule. Not only did John transfer immediately, but his generally outspoken manner was different from what I have seen in other African Kenyan clients. Through him I came to understand feelings and mechanisms which I can now discover more easily in clients who express themselves less clearly and which have helped me to understand myself better.

John also helped me to understand how important countertransference feelings are in understanding the patient and the dynamics in the treatment. Just because his talk about colonialism and exploitation made me so ill at ease, he continued talking about it. And as soon as I was able to address the issue and had asserted myself we dealt with it and the patient felt "healed."

Phase I

My first contact with John was when the office secretary asked me to take a new client who was in a very bad state. She explained how "bad" his state was by pointing out that he refused to leave the office when he was told after the intake interview that he "would hear from us." I agreed to see him, and that was the beginning of a brief but tumultuous therapy: sessions twice a week for a period of 3 months. Then he decided that he was "totally healed" and wanted to stop coming. We agreed that he would come once monthly for a while. He came back twice after a month's interval, but then decided very quickly that he could really live without me and went. At this moment of writing, almost a year has elapsed and I have not heard from him since.

In this case description I will focus on the phenomenon of transference and countertransference, omitting those aspects of his history, behavior, and feelings that are not directly related, but furnishing a little background information.

John is a single man in his mid-20s who works as a semi-skilled laborer. He comes to therapy because he is suffering from terrible fears of being seen, of being close to other people. These fears make him hide in cupboards at his place of work; boarding a bus is a nightmare to him; and he locks himself in his workshop so that he can leave after dark when nobody will see him. He feels people stare at him and laugh about him.

Right from the first session I find John a remarkable client who differs from most of my other clients. He talks freely and does not need encouragement to keep doing so for the full hour. When the time is up he is unwilling to leave, although I had explained to him at the beginning that the sessions would last one hour. When he gets the feeling I am really serious, he says he wants to come back the next day, although I had scheduled him for 2 hours a week and already told him the days. I give him a little piece of paper with my name (as a foreign name is usually difficult to remember), his client code number, and the time of his appointments, and I terminate the discussion.

My feelings at this stage were ambivalent. I was surprised when he did not want to leave and asked to see me every day. I had never had such an eager patient and I somewhat liked the idea of being wanted. On the other hand, I felt irritated; he clung to me too much and I felt like shaking him off.

He starts the second session by reporting that he feels really good about coming to see me. He had told everybody he met, he showed them the slip of paper with my name, and he and some friends even analyzed my writing.

"How nice, instant transference," says my supervisor.[1] But it does not feel nice to me: He already clings too much for my liking, will he now send all his friends to me, whom I imagine to be as creepy as I feel he is? I rationalize: They won't be on my private doorstep, but in the clinic; and, he is at least positive about coming to therapy.

In the next sessions he tries his best to control me. He wants me to advise him on going to work or not. He gives me piles of handwritten material but refuses to talk about what he wants me to do with it: Should I read it or what? He tells me I do not understand at all what he is feeling; if I did I would not ask him to come twice a week, because coming to the clinic is what he fears most. Why don't I give him drugs to make his fears disappear? He threatens me that he is going to kill himself and that would be my fault because I should have helped him more. He lingers around the center hours before and after his sessions, presumably hoping to get more than his scheduled time. He wants me to write him a note for his boss asking for sick leave, accuses me of forgetting everything, and snarls at me, "Do you people never take notes?"

He is trying to blackmail me with his suicide threat and I start feeling uncomfortable. When he again asks me to write a note for his boss to give him sick leave (which I do not want to do as it would only sanction his feeling sick), I tell him just to go to work so that we can talk about the feelings it arouses in him.

I realize I treat him as a 4-year-old: Don't whine, just go to work and we will talk about it later.

When he keeps asking for a note for his boss, I refer him to our clinical director, a psychiatrist and the person authorized to handle such matters. But no, John does not want this and instead accuses me of not being of any help. I should make the appointment with the clinical director for him; I am responsible for his cure as I am treating him.

I now tell him he is behaving like a 4-year-old and I give him all the examples of his clinging behavior from the previous sessions. "No, no," he says, "I am very mature," and he rationalizes all the examples that I had used to demonstrate his immaturity in order to prove the opposite.

I think: Good for you to resist me, but you have heard it all the same.

All this happened in the first four sessions and the fifth session he surprises me: He is 15 minutes late! When I ask him about it, he mentions oversleeping and problems with transport. I say, "Or do you mean you are feeling better and you can do without me?" John: "Yes indeed, I feel better." He had talked with his boss, who had not even noticed his absenteeism, which makes him feel very relieved.

He is still hiding from everyone "because they will laugh about me." He feels an absolutely inferior nobody. When I ask him who has planted that idea in his mind, he says, "Definitely my father, he wants me to buy a shamba [farmland], build a house, have Ksh 10,000/- in the bank; and I do not have anything like that at all, only dreams and a job I do not like." These dreams, which he will talk about very much later during his therapy, are about becoming a savior of the oppressed people of Kenya, becoming a politician, or writing books like Ngugi Wa'Thiongo,[2] books that will make the world think, will make them see all the injustices that happen everywhere.

His abundant talk about attending the treatment center and about everything that occupies him has alerted people in his place of work. His superiors arrange a visit to a psychiatrist for him. John is led to a psychiatric hospital for a consultation, whereupon he is prescribed loads of drugs, including major tranquilizers. On top of that, he is given 2 weeks sick leave, which is later even extended.

There is a strange contradiction in this exhibitionism: He fears focus on being with people and being laughed about; on the other hand he constantly invites people to react to him and, by being very challenging, encourages them to laugh about him. Later I will realize that this attitude of his misguided me for a while.

The next session is characterized by the fact that he is completely drugged. In reply to my question about the effectiveness of the drugs, he says: "They do not help at all, now I cannot think any more and that has always been the best thing I liked: to read and to think."

Then I ask him who he wants to be treated by, me or his psychiatrist? He reacts defensively; he does not want to stop seeing me. The psychiatrist has told him, "I treat the fears, let your therapist treat the causes." When I tell him it is difficult to treat somebody who cannot feel anything because of the drugs, he asks me, "Should I stop taking them?" and I tell him that is his decision, not mine. We agree that he will not take his medication just prior to therapy.

Throughout the following sessions he denies everything I tell him and tries to have me make decisions for him: Should he take the drugs or not; should he leave his job and devote his life to reading and thinking; should he continue schooling and try to finish his O-levels? He continues to blackmail me as he had endeavored to do at the beginning of therapy.

I reflect back to him how irresponsibly he behaves, tries to blackmail me, and gives me the feeling that he wants me to kick him out, to which he replies, "No, no, you cannot kick me out, I will stay for a whole year."

Privately I interpret his wish to stay as positive: He is giving me a chance to treat him properly and does not expect instant results.

As the psychiatrist he is seeing does not tell him anything and he is desperate to know what the drugs are "doing to him," he decides to make an appointment with our clinical director (after I had told him that I did not know much about medication and that he should consult him). I do not know what they talked about, but he reports, "This doctor is a very bad man. If I were you, I would dismiss him immediately."

At this stage we reach a turning point in the therapy.

I apparently frustrated his efforts to blackmail me and that did not frustrate him, but on the contrary gave him the confidence that I could stand his attacks. He almost seemed to reward me for my steadfastness by giving me more material. He very much gave me the feeling of testing me. For what purpose? Although it was never explicitly talked about in therapy, he consistently gave me the feeling that either his parents had used blackmail on him as a child, or he himself had used it as an effective device to get what he wanted. This irresponsible behavior seemed an integral part of his character. That I frustrated his efforts to get me down by this means must have been a great relief to him. While this behavior had brought him considerable "success" — he had even managed to get sick leave! — it had never given him confidence that he could rely on anybody. By yielding to his wishes they were also "lost" to him. It seems that he unconsciously tested me to decide, when he discovered that I did not yield, that it was safe enough to lift his defenses and to entrust more of his thoughts to me. He tested me to make sure I would not make the same mistake as other meaningful people in his life made. I passed the test when I showed him that I did not feel responsible for his suffering (see Gootnick, 1982).

Phase 2

John starts talking about what I privately label "politics." He opens with the statement that he feels all the Asians should be kicked out of the country immediately. If he were in power, he would do it instantaneously. To my question "Why?" he replies, "That is obvious, they monopolize the economy of the country, leaving no room for the real Kenyans, enriching themselves, exporting the money out of the country," and so forth.

I immediately feel furious; these generalized statements, these prejudices against ethnic groups enrage me.

Although he talks about "the Indians," I assume he means "the Whites" as well, and, being dependent on a permit myself, with the recurrent worry every year that it may not be extended, probably adds to my fury. As I am overwhelmed with anger, which I feel would not be therapeutic to ventilate, I choose to keep quiet, asking only little clarifications and encouraging him to go on. He does not need much encouragement and continues happily abusing everything that is not African and glorifying indigenous African culture in which there is "total harmony," as he tries to make me believe.

Probably because of lack of response from my side, John continues talking "politics" session after session: about the colonialists, how bad they were, oppressing people in a country that was not theirs; how ridiculous it is that they claim to have "discovered" Kenya while the Kenyans had lived there for ages and knew all the places and knew that their gods were born there. Again he tells me that he would like all the Asians kicked out of the country today— preferably yesterday—because they monopolize the trade; actually all the Whites should be kicked out as well. He talks about how he admires Ngugi Wa'Thiongo and would like to write as he does; that he actually started writing a novel and would like to go on with it; that this first novel was a Western-oriented "James Hadley Chase"[3] type novel and that now he would like to write one much more Africa-oriented.

Having given both his criticism and its transference implications some thought, I start finding it easier to comment. I recognize that his criticism is right in a lot of ways. When he refers directly to the Colonials, I tell him I am also a representative of the Whites, and when he declares "all the Whites out," I say, "then I would be gone as well."

Interspersed with his talk about politics, another theme that comes up is his worry about his small body size. He comes with the confession that he thinks his penis is "negligibly small." One day a girl remarked that she could not understand how he could "manage."

His actual sexual life is by no means a series of disasters, although he has never had a long-lasting relationship. But concern about his "negligible" penis is still there. John does not want to wash himself in the public bathroom of his compound for fear people will see it and he is absolutely sure that many are desperate to catch a glimpse of it. I relate this to his fears (and his unconscious wish) of being seen by people, which indeed focus on women, and I tell him that he seems to treat his penis as if it equals his whole person, as if he himself is absolutely negligible.

It is remarkable that at this point he touches upon more intimate aspects of his life. He seems to treat therapy as a hurdle race: Whenever he feels that I have taken an obstacle successfully, he will reward me with more relevant material, at the same time using it as another test, to see whether he can still trust me.

Although he keeps talking "politics," his tone is changing. He not only shows anger about all the injustice that goes on everywhere, but relates fantasies about the role he would like to play coming to the rescue of the oppressed. He admires Ngugi Wa'Thiongo, wonders what he would have to do to become like him. He compares himself with Karega, one of the main characters in Ngugi's novel *Petals of Blood*, the teacher who becomes a unionist and leads his friends in their protest against neo-Colonial injustice.

In the beginning John never reacted to my comments that I would be gone as well, when he advocated purging the country of Indians and Whites. Now he says, "Your case can be reconsidered." Talking about his psychiatrist, he suddenly mentions a different name, so I ask him whether he has changed. He thinks a while, then says, "No, you are OK, I was mixing up the names, it was always the same. You have a very good memory!"

But still he makes me feel ill at ease. I immediately feel guilt for all that my Dutch ancestors have done, not here but in Indonesia. I seem to agree with his unspoken assumption that I am related to all sorts of Colonialists and see myself as representing the oppressing classes. At the same time I think, "What nonsense, I did nothing at all to harm you! I do not have to feel guilty for what other people did long ago and are still doing."

As a result of this I tell him that he is making the situation difficult for me: I am supposed to help him, but he continually puts me in the position of the accused.

To ease my ill feelings (and maybe even more because I want to be liked by him), I respond when John asks me questions about whether I know Ngugi Wa'Thiongo and read his novels. "Yes," I say, "I read them"; and when he mentions titles I confirm having read them, which is indeed true. I am surprised at how much he has read, not only Kenyan writers, but also Nigerian and other West African authors. When I acknowledge having read Ngugi, he says, "Well, that is nice of you, at least you try, but you will never be able to understand it." I agree with him, yes, indeed I am the wrong color and I cannot manage to change it. But at the same time I resent saying that, instead of expressing my irritation about the fact that whatever I do, it is wrong in his eyes.

At this point I also have to restrain myself from asking too many questions about what he thinks about all sorts of books. It could easily have developed into a Literary Circle in which we discussed African literature, but which probably would have had slight therapeutic value.

Although I took his criticism of the Colonials and everything that is connected with it seriously—I could see that he was right in a lot of ways, that there were good grounds for his criticism—I did not sense the depth of John's feelings in relation to his political statements. As a result, the atmosphere when talking about these things had always been quite light-hearted.

Then, just "by coincidence," I started reading some novels of Andre Brink: first *The Wall of the Plague* (1984), then *An Instant in the Wind* (1976). The latter especially made me think of Doris Lessing's (1950/1980) book, *The Grass Is Singing*, a book I read years ago, about black-white relations in what was then called Rhodesia, which made a great impact on me. I remember the frightening, sinister atmosphere that it described which I recognized again in *An Instant in the Wind* and later also in Coetzee's (1983) *Dusklands*: the contempt, the disdain of Whites toward Blacks, the humiliations the Blacks endured.

I suddenly got the feeling that I had to take his political talk far more seriously in the light of his intense feelings of humiliation, frustration, anger, and inferiority; and that these feelings were probably more deeply embedded in his personality than I would expect political ideologies to be. I realize now that his exhibitionistic way of exposing himself that I had described earlier also contributed to my late realization of his intense feelings.

My feelings when treating him change considerably in this period. I start to understand his anger better and feel less threatened by it. The more I see it as a serious problem he is struggling with, the less I have to see it as something directed to *me*. So I become at once more and less detached and my interventions become directed at therapeutic effect instead of "life-saving" devices for me.

In these sessions during which he is talking about politics, he returns every now and then to asking me what he should do. I tell him that he is digging a pitfall for me: He tries to lure me into telling him what to do, and as soon as I do so, he will tell me that I am a terrible imperialistic colonialist who wants to prescribe him what to do. I tell him I do not want to fall into his trap and that he should take responsibility for his own life.

The Third Month — Termination of Therapy

John initiates all sorts of actions. He experiments in dispensing with his medication; he looks for advice about how to become a publishable writer; he meets with some University staff who advise him to start studying for O and A levels privately, after which he could join the University; he then subscribes to a correspondence course to complete his O-levels. He also considers the possibility of joining a diploma course which he has been offered by his employers. He finds it rather uninteresting but can see that it might lead to better pay and general advancement.

But he does not regard financial betterment as important; it will only drive him away from his ideal of being one with the poor. He is also worried that this therapy is going to turn him into an "ordinary" person who has no ideals anymore, and that is the last thing he wants to happen. When I ask him whether he has the feeling that I want him to become ordinary, he says he is not sure. "No," he grants that, "you do not press me, but one never knows . . . "

He is still seeing the psychiatrist who keeps changing his prescription. He is curious and worried about what these drugs are doing to him, and, as I told him already, I do not know much about it. He decides to consult our clinical director again. Our CD informs him about direct effects and side effects and tells him that he can experiment with the dosage himself, thus again stressing his own responsibility.

He starts missing whole sessions and comes late because of oversleeping. His explanation is that now that he has stopped taking his medication he falls asleep very late at night and then does not wake up in the morning.

He tells me how he fell in love with a woman at work, some 10 years older than he is, how he tried to see her as much as he could, liked to hear her voice, and so forth. As I am also about 10 years older, I ask him whether he feels in love with me. "No, that is a very silly idea, that could never come to my mind, you are my doctor."

When he is again very late I remark, "You do not seem to feel like coming anymore." John answers, "Oh no, I just overslept. I feel much better, I am healed." When I ask him whether he oversleeps because he has the feeling he does not need to come anymore, he agrees; indeed, he has decided to stop coming.

I have the feeling that he is making very quick decisions, without involving me in the process. When I confront him with that he tells me that he has thought about it for a long time; he has also decided to stop seeing the psychiatrist and tore up his hospital card. He feels he can deal with his problems if they ever come back and he wants to use his money for other purposes.

As I like his decisive spirit and see that he might disappear forever if I try to force him to stay, I offer him a free session in a month's time. He eagerly agrees to that, saying he likes coming and talking but that he cannot afford to pay the money for something he does not really need, but only likes.

The next appointment is for the end of the month and John comes almost half an hour late. He says he feels bad; had a quarrel with his girlfriend and kicked her out just the evening before. I am surprised, "I did not know you had a girlfriend."

J: Well, I've had one for 3 weeks.
I: That is curious. And when you come to see me you feel you do not need her any longer.
J: No, that is nonsense.

We talk about the girlfriend and John's ambivalent feelings toward her and I relate it to the transference. John says his girlfriend is very stupid and low class and that is why he feels so ashamed that he kicked her out. Had she been more upper class it would have been OK. But she forced him to do so; she behaved in a silly manner, let herself be swung round by other men and such a thing cannot be tolerated in his culture. He likes best to stay in bed with her for the whole day and just talk. I ask him whether she liked that as well. "No," he says, "she is too stupid, no brains, she just says uh, uh." I reply, "That is just like me, I often say no more than uh, uh." John answers, "Well, at least you have read Ngugi."

He also mentions that as usual he had been talking about going to see me and how good it is, when the person he was talking with told him that he had also been seeing a therapist. This man had been in one of the groups that were run in the clinic and he told my client that he had not liked it. It had been very strange, just talking; he had dropped out after three sessions. But miraculously, after that he had never suffered from his complaints again! My client immediately takes this as another example that shows how wonderful this sort of therapy is, and adds, "You know, this man did not know anything about psychology. That is why he did not understand what was happening."

Then he asks me what the group this man mentioned is about and I explain briefly what it entails. He wants to know who is running it and I tell him it is Dr. X. He says, "Well, I do not know that man." I tell him that he knows him, "He is our clinical director, you talked with him and suggested to me that we should dismiss him." He is flabbergasted!

When he continues to speak about the man who thought that his "cure" had nothing to do with the therapy I seize the opportunity to remind him that he also always denied any link between his improvement and his therapy; he always liked talking to me but it did not help him.

One month later he returns; the situation with his girlfriend is worrying him. Although he kicked her out, he cannot stop thinking about her; he wants to go away from Nairobi to think about everything calmly on his own. He is afraid he may relapse again and raises the issue of coming back regularly. I tell him he is welcome to return if he feels he needs it. We agree on an appointment in the following week.

Although we had tentatively agreed that this would be the first session of John's second period of coming regularly, he had decided in the meantime that this should really be the end. He had been away for the week, stayed in a rural town in his home area; everybody spoke his tribal language over there and he had enjoyed not hearing any English or Kiswahili.

About his job, he remarks that he still does not like it. But in a very matter-of-fact tone he adds, "But of course I'll stay there until I have found something else." I do not mention that I consider this a good decision, as I'm afraid he will interpret it with, "You see, you want me to become ordinary." At the same time I feel it is good that he can apparently distinguish between liking to do more interesting things and seeing it would be foolish to throw away the only security he has.

His last message is that he compares himself with Okonkwo, the main character in Chinua Achebe's (1962) novel, *Things Fall Apart*. As I do not remember the plot of this novel well, he explains: Okonkwo prefers to hang himself rather than adopt Western ideas!

DISCUSSION

As I wanted to discuss the special problems that can arise in cross-cultural therapies, I focused the description of this case on the issues that specifically referred to our cross-cultural setting. In reality John spent more time talking about his problems with women and about his upbringing than this paper reflects.

The patient was remarkable in many ways, not the least in the fact that he never avoided commenting on my alleged behavior. In the beginning he was full of ambivalence: He liked coming, felt really good when talking with me, however I should help him more. I was just another Colonialist and could never understand people with his color, and so forth. During the therapy he became more and more positive toward me: In the beginning he commented that I "just forget"; later he praised my good memory. Although of course I am the wrong color, he later said that he could reconsider my position when he wanted to kick out all the Whites. He also saw my reading of Ngugi as a positive point. And when he stopped coming regularly, he needed a girlfriend to replace me! He even became more positive toward the clinic: Dr. X., who should be dismissed at first, later turned out to be not all that bad.

But his last message must not be misunderstood: Like Okonkwo, he would prefer to hang himself rather than surrender to his therapist!

Of course, this change took place gradually and manifested itself in all sorts of little interactions. For example, one day my watch had stopped, so I had to ask him the time. He was amazed that I had a watch that did not function. He expressed his surprise: He thought that all Whites had expensive watches that never failed! On the other hand, I recognized his jealousy that I was in a position to work for nothing (he knew about the voluntary nature of the center), that is, just because I liked it.

As for the countertransference, my initial feelings of being ill at ease, despairing, worried, merit examination. I took them as a response to his inductions to feel responsible for his cure. I realized I did not have to feel responsible if I dealt with these feelings therapeutically and resisted being trapped by his dependent projections.

I attribute these countertransference feelings mainly to the fact that I am just beginning my work as a therapist. At that time I had 2 years experience in this field and I see these problems as relating to technique.

More fundamental were my feelings induced by John's direct political attacks on my integrity. My whole background of sociological studies, which so strongly emphasized how the "experts" in development "aid" often turn out to be neo-Colonialists who brainwash the people, came into the picture. In addition, my colonial cultural heritage compelled serious search of my own conscience. The fact that I indeed replied to his searching questions of what I read was definitely inspired by my motives to look better than those he condemned. This feeling was probably also responsible for my renewed interest in reading about race relations in Africa.

His general, undifferentiated attacks on everything and everybody that is not black and African also made me very angry. It made me resentful and induced me to think of him as a ruthless person.

My reading of pro-African writers, mixed with the biweekly attacks, turned out to be a useful combination. I started to understand the background of his feelings, to see the depth of them. But I also recognized my own anger as partly justifiable and not as something that had to be denied out of misplaced superiority feelings. I came to the point that I could acknowledge his feelings toward Colonialists, Whites, and expatriates without feeling guilty and without feeling so attacked and angry that I could no longer deal with them therapeutically.

The fact that I am writing a paper about John is probably an indication of the strong feelings I had and still have toward him. Both of us seemed to try to impress each other by presenting ourselves as different from our groups, John by presenting his idealistic ideas and all he had read and by remarks like "I know about psychology so I understand, but others . . . ," while I tried a bleak defense against his attacks by assuring him that I really read. . . .

So far we both seem to have benefited. John was restored to acceptable social functioning and his fears became manageable. I gained a clearer sense of my own position as an expatriate in a foreign country and started feeling much more free. So it shows that although cross-cultural situations in therapy pose specific and additional problems to the therapy, they can be dealt with and, if this is done successfully, are of great benefit to both the client and the therapist.

NOTES

1. Mrs. Marie Coleman Nelson, without whom this paper would never have been written and whom I would like to thank very much for her encouraging support.
2. Ngugi Wa'Thiongo, a Kenyan author, writing politically inspired novels, mainly to address neo-colonial tendencies in Kenyan society, presently living in self-imposed exile in Great Britain.
3. James Hadley Chase, author of cheap thrillers, sold by the millions in Africa.

REFERENCES

Achebe, C. (1962). *Things fall apart*. Heinemann African Writers Series.
Brink, A. (1976). *An instant in the wind*. W.H. Allen & Co.
Brink, A. (1984). *The wall of the plague*. London: Faber & Faber.
Coetzee, J.M. (1983). *Dusklands*. London: Penguin Books.
Gootnick, I. (1982). The problem of treating an intensely suffering patient: To gratify or to frustrate? *Psychoanalytic Review, 69*(4).
Gorkin, M. (1986). Countertransference in cross cultural psychotherapy: The example of Jewish therapist and Arab patient. *Psychiatry, 49*(1).
Gorkin, M., Masalha, S., & Yativ, G. (1985). Psychotherapy of Israeli-Arab patients: Some cultural considerations. *The Journal of Psychoanalytic Anthropology, 8*(4).
Lessing, D. (1980). *The grass is singing*. Grafton Books. (Original work published 1950.)
Nelson, M.C. (1987). Immunization factors in development of the African personality: Preliminary observations. *Psychoanalytic Review, 74*(2).
Ngugi Wa'Thiongo. (1977). *Petals of blood*. Heinemann African Writers Series.

Fighting the War
from Behind Barbed Wire:
Psychotherapy in a Juvenile
Detention Facility

Sanford S. Fishbein
Richard R. Kilburg

SUMMARY. The work of a psychotherapist inside a juvenile detention facility is explored. Referral issues, presenting problems, unique psychodynamics, substance abuse patterns, and family histories of the principally poor, black, male, adolescent residents are presented. Transference and countertransference issues are described. Case illustrations are provided to highlight and articulate therapeutic issues.

Sanford S. Fishbein, PhD, received his Doctoral degree in Counseling Psychology from the University of Notre Dame in 1986. He has held positions at the Psychological Sciences Institute and at Koba Associates. He is currently the lead psychologist in "The Detention Center Project" for the Health Department of Prince George's County, MD. He has several publications in the areas of learning and social attribution. Mailing address: Outreach Services, 6490G Landover Rd., Landover, MD 20785.

Richard R. Kilburg, PhD, received his Doctoral degree in Clinical Psychology from the University of Pittsburgh in 1972. He has held positions in the Department of Psychiatry at the University of Pittsburgh, the Champlain Mental Health Council, the American Psychological Association, and Psychological Sciences Institute. He is currently Director of the Faculty and Staff Assistance Program at The Johns Hopkins University and Hospital in Baltimore. He has published a number of articles and book chapters and is the senior editor of "Psychologists in Distress: Issues, Syndromes, and Solutions in Psychology" published by the American Psychological Association. Mailing address: Suite 508, 550 North Broadway, Baltimore, MD 21205.

105

Working as a psychotherapist in a juvenile detention facility is in many ways like providing services in a Mobile Army Surgical Hospital (MASH) near the front lines of a battle zone. In this case, the war is being fought in the streets of the American ghetto. The soldiers are young men who come to our facility gaunt and battle weary. Some are dazed, bloodied, and wounded. Crisis management and triage are the major tasks. The former implies the need for flexibility and energy. The latter can be more frustrating, as triage is traditionally considered to be the first step in the provision of services necessary to heal the individual. In our setting, subsequent services are not often delivered, leading almost inevitably to recidivism. Longer-term work, to induce insight and produce behavioral change, usually is not possible due to the exigencies of the situation.

A confounding factor is that frequently these soldiers do not desire our services. Tolerating frustration, battling anger and resentment, and coping with shame all become integral parts of the job of therapists in these institutions. Multiple problems are encountered, and occur on intrapersonal, interpersonal, institutional, systemic, cultural, and societal levels. Interventions tailored to remedy a difficulty at one level often fail due to a lack of foresight and understanding of the interrelationships, or because these levels are unreachable by interventions of the institutional psychotherapist.

The purposes of this paper are to review the types of problems encountered by psychotherapists working with poor, inner-city youths in detention settings; to describe the psychodynamics, transference and countertransference issues most often encountered; and to offer suggestions about the types of therapeutic approaches that can be used effectively with this population.

THE SERVICE SETTING

The present institution serves as a jail and holding facility for male juveniles generally between 13 and 18 years of age who are alleged to have committed serious crimes. Approximately half of the population have been committed there by the courts, while the other half are detained, awaiting judicial proceedings. Over the previous 12 months, the population was about 98.5% Black, 1% Hispanic, and 0.5% White. The average number of residents usually exceeds 200, 33% over the maximum 150 youths the facility was designed to hold. Of the committed adolescents, the most common convictions are for drug, weapon, and automobile charges, followed by assaults, burglaries, and robberies.

The facility itself has been ordered closed by the courts because of its age and its physical inadequacies. Since greater numbers of adolescents continue to be arrested for the commission of increasingly serious and violent crimes, the facility must remain open. Adequate alternatives to placement there do not exist. An ongoing compromise is being hammered out by the local government and the courts. Institutional changes have been put into place in an attempt to meet the standards of previous court rulings. This has been quite difficult, for the local government has been naturally reluctant to commit funds to a facility about to be closed down.

The residents of the institution are serviced by three psychologists. Responsibilities for a particular boy depends upon which of the seven cottages he lives in. To simplify procedures, once a resident has worked with a psychologist, that psychologist continues to provide services unless a transfer is made, even if the boy is moved to a cottage which is covered by a colleague.

REFERRAL FOR TREATMENT

Residents are referred for psychotherapy in a variety of ways. Some youth come to the facility with judicial orders for psychotherapy, because the court has had problems with the adolescent and/or his family, either during or before his trial. Sometimes, a judge will be apprised by social workers or probation officers of significant difficulties within a multi-problem family, and will order psychotherapy while the youth is being held. These orders can be for treatment as a condition of incarceration, or to obtain an expert opinion on the desirability of residential placement if the youth is found guilty and committed to the system.

Frequently, staff members will refer a resident. Usually, it is because he has been acting out in some troublesome manner, most typically not following directions and thereby enticing others to do likewise. At times, an adolescent will be referred for threatening suicide. Most often, such a threat is a manipulative attempt to secure a more favorable living placement, or privileges like a home visit. Sometimes, however, it is a reality-based response to his current, hopeless life situation.

Occasionally, a youth will self-refer for therapy, particularly after he has seen the psychotherapist working with his peers for a time. While about half of these self-requests are manipulative attempts to secure privileges already disallowed by staff (e.g., extra telephone calls, minimum-security placement), about half are appropriate cries for help.

Finally, a few adolescents will solicit help without asking directly for it. They always say hello, greeting the psychotherapist, and making small talk. Eventually, those behaviors may evolve into a request for treatment. The adolescents' self-requests are quite remarkable. Speaking to a psychotherapist can elicit stigmatizing comments from their tough, adolescent, male peers. As they are pulled for therapy from daily activities such as school, other boys will often hoot, "Yeah, talk to him; he's crazy!"

PROBLEMS PRESENTED BY THE RESIDENTS

Although rarely articulated by the adolescents as a presenting problem, anxiety is often behaviorally manifested in the form of lack of concentration, restlessness, sleeplessness, and so on. On one level, this can be considered a positive prognostic sign, as the more sociopathic residents with longer records of more violent crimes do not seem to be as troubled by their circumstances. They might be more accurately characterized as annoyed by their incarceration and frustrated by the interruptions in their lives.

Typically, these incarcerated adolescents are from families with many problems. Substance abuse, poverty, and physical abuse are common concerns for the boys. Despite these adolescents' apparent inadequacies interpersonally and scholastically, quite often they are important sources of family income. Often they participate in illegal activities like drug dealing and car theft for quick monetary gain that is usually shared within the family.

Anxiety may be further exacerbated to the extent that the child perceives himself to be the sole physical protector of the family.

The physical risks for many of these urban ghetto families are real. The incarceration in these cases can cause overwhelming anxiety because family members can be hurt or killed if they are not with the adolescent.

A clear example of this is seen in the case of Donnell, who was very anxious. His behaviors resulted in complaints from each of the staff members he encountered. He was viewed as "hyperactive," unable to respond to them like the other boys. The most common adjective used to describe Donnell was "limited." It was clear that most of the staff thought that his intellectual functioning was borderline or mildly retarded. When the therapist talked to him, Donnell stated that he was actually responsible for the daily functioning of his family. He cooked, cleaned, washed, and shopped. He was the caretaking rudder for his substance-abusing family. He vehemently denied that there were problems at home. His anxiety would overwhelm him as he imagined his loved ones attempting to cope with the family business and informal relationships without him there to smooth things. Almost none of the institutional staff would accept the role this young man played in his family, since it was so discrepant with his behavior while at the institution.

Before incarceration, the boys manage much of this anxiety by continual movement and energy deployment into new social and criminal endeavors. In the institution, they are frequently confined to one room. This forces many of them to think about previously unresolved personal and family issues that they have successfully avoided in the past. Anxiety levels can become so great that reports of auditory and visual hallucinations are common.

Depression is a second frequent complaint in this incarcerated population. Sleep disruptions, including insomnia or oversleeping, chronic fatigue, loss of appetite, and social isolation are the most common symptoms. Depression is probably underreported, because the depressed youth is less likely to reach out and request to speak to someone. In addition, staff may be less likely to report them because, by and large, these children are not problematic. They do what they are told, keep to themselves, and are quiet and sleepy during the day.

At times, the depression is of recent origin, relating to the separation from loved ones that incarceration necessitates. The residents experience quick multiple losses: their social role within their peer group, school, and family; their familial role as physical and financial protector; and the emotional support that family and friends provide. Greater numbers of angry, acting-out, suicide threats and gestures come from these situationally depressed children.

More frequently, the symptoms are caused by chronic depression related to unresolved conflicts and issues of historical and developmental importance. Most often these involve the loss of a parent. Usually the losses were abrupt and/or violent, including incarceration and murder. Mourning is seldom completed. These children *look* sad. Time has forced them to accept these events as *faits accomplis*. However, such losses usually cause great disruption and chaos in the families.

The boys then attempt to numb themselves to the pain. The families may attempt to withdraw socially and culturally. Most often the families do not discuss what and why it happened, compounding the problem and serving to further repress the confusing and hurtful feelings. A code of silence is maintained. The boy knows that he feels awful, but because of a lack of acknowledgment that such feelings are appropriate and permissible, he becomes stoic, and often guilty and ashamed for possessing them. In addition, humiliation can be exacerbated by the cause of the loss, as in a case where a father was killed while selling drugs. These feelings of shame and guilt can make boys feel vulnerable in the war zone of the streets, where such emotions can be very risky. Therefore, it is quite common to see such feelings defended by rage, which is much more functional in the battle on the streets. The chronically depressed adolescents will more readily admit to suicidal ideation. These thoughts can function as an escape hatch through which they have the freedom to travel. In this situation, suicide becomes the ultimate assertion of volitional control.

Physical complaints also come to the attention of the psychotherapist. The boys are often suffering from a frequently unspecified physical symptom. Upon investigation, these adolescents are invariably attempting to cope with a number of life difficulties, any one of which would be sufficient cause to seek therapy. The reticence to call for help may be age, race, or culturally related. Talking about themselves and their concerns was not learned at home. They do not expect to solve their problems. These adolescents have learned that trouble, in one form or another, is *always* present. Nothing short of divine intervention is expected to alter this inevitability. Therapy is also interpreted in the same nonefficacious terms.

Finally, some presenting concerns are related to organic problems. Origins include genetics, head injuries both from accidents and physical abuse, and maternal substance abuse during pregnancy. Usually, these issues come to light indirectly, as the result of psychological testing. Further neurological testing is performed if such organic concerns are identified. This can be quite a problem, as services may not be obtainable on-grounds, because of a lack of equipment and/or trained assessors. Off-grounds assessment requires co-ordination with outside resources, and raises the possibility that the youth will escape. Even if the evaluation is obtained, it is unlikely that anything will be done about the problems, as remedial services at the institution are always in short supply.

PROVIDING SERVICES

Although the role of a psychologist/psychotherapist can be a multifaceted one, primarily, it is restricted to that of expert consultant. Process consultation is usually employed in cases involving youths in crises, those needing psychiatric monitoring, disciplinary problems, and residents acting out in various ways. As a consultant, the psychotherapist is expected to perform individual, family, and group psychotherapy in both short-term and long-term formats. Also included in the role are crisis intervention and psychological evaluations for treatment, court evaluations, and assessments for placement into other institutions. Finally, as part of a multidisciplinary treatment team, the psychotherapist participates by offering opinions as to the most efficacious course of treatment for residents and for appropriate placement out of the facility.

Performing psychotherapy with the population of a juvenile detention facility calls for an eclectic approach. Healing the wounds of these adolescents requires flexibility, because you are never quite sure at the outset of the cause, extent, and severity of the previous trauma, and whether the boy will be amenable to treatment. A combination of psychodynamic, behavioral, and client-centered methods in a variety of formats is necessary.

These children are masters at denying the discomfort of their problems. They generally see no need to examine themselves or their lives. For day-to-day living, their denial is their most useful survival mechanism. Persistence on the part of the therapist in the face of this massive denial is a prerequisite for working with this population.

Reality Therapy

Techniques of reality therapy are essential. Confrontation is the most important way to catalyze change. This typically involves the repeated identification of problem situations in which the youngster frequently finds himself. Inevitably, the youngster will deny any problem, or detail the unreasonableness of the other person(s) involved without mentioning any of his own culpability. If you work with similar populations, you will undoubtedly find yourself pounding away at the fact that regardless of past life or current situations, first and foremost, the youngster must take responsibility for the outcomes of his actions. This is a necessary condition for significant and long-standing behavioral change.

Client-Centered Therapy

Supportive methods, such as those advocated by Jourard (1964), are often quite helpful in building rapport with the residents. Of primary importance is the self-disclosure of the "transparent" psychotherapist. Much acceptance of the normality and propriety of feelings and anxiety will occur as the result of such self-disclosure. For example, the psychotherapist can acknowledge and express irritation at repeated interruptions of the therapy session. Positive modeling is also facilitated. This may be especially true when there is greater dissimilarity in background and experiences between the psychotherapist and the residents such as when a therapist is of a different race. Many of these adolescents have never spent time with adults who can express feelings like anger or anxiety without becoming violent, or sadness without becoming depressed. Their experiences have been with adults who are often substance abusing, noncommunicative, and exploitative. Therefore, a psychotherapist who is both accepting of his or her own feelings, and willing to discuss them is both educational and therapeutic, aiding both self-acceptance and self-understanding.

Behavior Therapy

Acting out must be dealt with behaviorally, through the judicious use of positive and negative reinforcement. Punishment should be avoided, as it is less effective. By withdrawing and supplying reinforcements, privileges like extra time out of their rooms, telephone calls, and so on, socially acceptable behaviors can be shaped rapidly, especially when the requirements are explained in a nonjudgmental manner devoid of anger. Except for psychotic episodes, reinforcement is usually sufficient for eliciting desired behaviors. Finally, operant conditioning in the form of the psychotherapist's approval as the youngster moves toward more appropriate behaviors can be critical.

Brief Psychotherapy

The principles and aims of short-term psychodynamic psychotherapy are very useful for the psychotherapist in this setting. Although the characteristics of the adolescent delinquent population are very different than the selection criteria advocated for brief psychotherapy patients (Marmor, 1979), the goals and time constraints are the same. These boys generally do not possess high ego strength, demonstrate the capacity to trust other human beings, stay in touch with their emotions, or have keen insight about their unconscious drives like the most desirable brief psychotherapy patients. In addition, their motivation to work and to change may be poor.

However, techniques that foster the appropriate release of tension, the hope for a solution, the help of a professional adult, insight, and a therapeutic alliance can be useful. The continual focus on the critical core issue to the exclusion of less important concerns can be an effective antidote to their denial. The high level of activity and involvement on the part of the psychotherapist that short-term work necessitates (Bauer & Kobos, 1987), demonstrates that someone important obviously does care.

CONFIDENTIALITY ISSUES

In providing services to this population, two questions frequently arise with regard to privileged information. First, what information gained in therapy should be shared with staff in related disciplines working as a team with the youth? Second, how should information learned from other staff be handled? Confidential information within the milieu should be used to educate other staff, so that those working with the boy can have more understanding about the boy's behavior. The nature and extent of the disclosure should be limited, however, so that the information is the minimum amount required to improve their knowledge. Of course, the psychotherapist should clearly and carefully explain the limits on confidentiality before beginning psychotherapy with the adolescent.

At certain times, material is obtained from staff as a consequence of sharing information with them. For example, only by disclosing some information to staff can the psychotherapist learn that the dying relative to whom the youngster refers in treatment sessions passed away years before. Although the psychotherapist is being tested and needs to behave "as if" (i.e., treating the boy's pronouncements as fact, in order that trust be built, dignity be maintained, and the need to hide due to humiliation be respected), this piece of information received from a colleague creates very different meanings for the therapy sessions. Such sharing among staff is sometimes essential, given the degree of manipulativeness and lying that is encountered in this population.

When using information obtained from other sources, you must be careful about pacing in treatment. It is likely that in the course of making a referral for psychotherapy, the staff member will share information about the youth to demonstrate the propriety of the referral. Lack of sensitivity to its disclosure may cause increased resistance and may cost the psychotherapist valuable time and information. If you move too fast, the youth responds as if he has been stripped naked and robbed of the structure that allows him to function as a respected, social, human being. By not respecting his right to share himself at a pace with which he feels comfortable, you run the risk of committing psychological rape. He may have to "lie still and take it," but further cooperation will not be forthcoming. This pacing issue is critical given the time pressure under which the therapists in this setting frequently work.

An example of improper pacing occurred with Damon, who was seen by a psychotherapist in his office. The previous night, he had been the victim of an alleged sexual assault. Earlier that day, he had gotten into a fight with another resident while playing basketball. During the initial interview, he patiently answered questions about the incident and the fight, and then requested and executed telephone calls to his grandmother and lawyer. After the calls, the psychotherapist tried to obtain some historical data to fill in the gaps of the information that he had already received from Damon's social worker.

Attempting to test some hypotheses, the therapist's questions became increasingly personal and intrusive. For example, the psychotherapist asked about the details of a previous sodomy complaint against Damon and his brother. Damon became angrier. Suddenly, Damon asked the questioner if he was a psychologist. The therapist replied in the affirmative. Damon then angrily exclaimed that he did not have any problems. When the therapist disagreed, pointing to the most recent events in support of this conclusion, Damon got up and walked out of the office.

The next day, Damon was brought to the psychotherapist's office by his social worker. His face was swollen from a fight in which he had been knocked unconscious by another resident. After explaining the sketchy details of the fight, which was the carryover of a "street beef," Damon stated again that he had no problems, and did not need to speak with a psychologist. When confronted with the fact that some kind of difficulty was occurring as the events of the previous 48 hours were recounted, he again walked out of the psychotherapist's office.

The following day, Damon was again brought to the psychotherapist's office by his social worker. This time, there had been a fight at school, and again the circumstances were similar: Another gang member had remembered Damon's role in a shooting, and had punched him unconscious. When Damon saw the psychotherapist, he turned his head away, stating that he did not like him, had no problems, and would not speak to him. Damon was transferred from the institution later that day. Had he stayed, a transfer to another therapist may have been necessary, due to the premature confrontation about his problems and ineffective coping skills that had alienated Damon. Greater patience on the part of the therapist might have allowed Damon to acknowledge that he did indeed have problems that needed to be addressed.

PSYCHODYNAMIC ISSUES

Psychodynamically, many of these adolescents come from families where they appear to have won the oedipal struggle (R.G.K. Kainer, personal communication, March 1985; Kohut, 1979). The typical family constellation involves an absent father, a mother, parents and siblings of her nuclear family, and the boy's other siblings. Often the adolescent has been the most enduring and significant male in his mother's life. In fact, their ages might not be much different, as many of the residents' mothers started to have children in their early to mid-teens. Therefore, their relationship takes on many of the emotional characteristics of a marriage. Of course, these youth are ill equipped to cope with the psychological consequences of such a relationship. Mothers become too dependent, relying on them to fulfill their own "deficiency needs" (Maslow, 1968). Indeed, often teenage mothers report that a primary reason for having children is so that someone will love them (Dash, 1989).

As their relationship evolves, the boy starts by providing physical comfort, and eventually, he becomes a psychological caretaker. In some families, the youth becomes the main financial support and physical protector as well. As his importance within the family grows, so does his influence on the limits placed on his behaviors. Increasingly, normal parenting decisions are turned over to him, as if he were an adult. The impact that such an environment has on a boy is enormous.

When the boy is on the brink of manhood in adolescence, a competing male often enters the picture as a paramour or stepfather. Our conqueror, unopposed since infancy, is swiftly supplanted just at the time that he has begun to separate from the family and venture out on his own. The lesson learned is that if he leaves, he gets discarded. Depending on the youngster's level of individuation, two responses are likely: (1) either total separation, where the youth, rejected, goes on to live his own life; or, (2) he comes running back, demanding the safety of the previous emotional fusion. In either case, the result is the same, as he attempts to cope with rejection and abandonment by the mother.

The psychodynamic picture that emerges is one of an oedipal conqueror, who by winning actually loses. In victory, he loses an important source for the development of his own superego. The absence of a strong male figure to align with his mother, whose presence would reinforce that there are certain things which the boy should not have or do, impairs the development of an internal mechanism that provides a similar limit-setting function.

"Losing" his mother to a new rival, the boy begins to act out in antisocial patterns which reveal his rage. Not only does this acting out not win her back, it often drives her farther away as he becomes unmanageable. Frustration mounts for both synergistically. The boy goes out on the street, having been psychologically kicked out of the nest. Rejected by his mother for another suitor, ashamed because such a rejection implies defectiveness, weakness, and inadequacy, and enraged at his circumstances, he turns outward, missing the internal control of a well developed superego—another ideal recruit for the street wars. Strong parenting figures that consistently delimited right from wrong could help him survive such a crisis. The boy's increasingly criminal behavior reveals that he is out of control and that internal controls are deficient.

In the more extreme cases, where significant personal trauma was more deleterious, and in a culture where violence is increasingly acceptable, the murder of "identity-less" others becomes a behavioral option. For these adolescents, the experience of being raised in a dysfunctional family where unpredictability reigned increases the probability that they will become impulsive children. They learn that immediate gratification is necessary, because delay often means loss.

With their startlingly low self-esteem, reinforced by almost daily parental "abandonment," these boys care little about what the authorities can do to them as they are destroying themselves. Time and again they will verbalize the fact that "you can't hurt me." Given their life experiences, their assessment of what the authorities do to them is accurate when they weigh the threatened punishment of loss of privileges or liberty against the daily experience of social and family systems that are murdering their human spirit. They are at war both internally and in the streets, and will often kill others in "self-defense."

What these children have learned in abandonment is that they are unworthy of being loved. Ashamed of their rejection, the loss brings grief and mourning. Essentially told that they are unlovable, they are also deprived of people to love. Certainly, murder comes more easily to adolescents who were never loved, nor permitted to love. The impact on their self-esteem is crushing. These unloved adolescents are abandoned by their parents, and then by society, as social institutions like school and church fail them. As they are repeatedly told that they are unwanted, useless, dirty failures, they become frozen in a "Mask of Shame" (Wurmser, 1981). The most frequent defensive response is rage. It surrounds them with an invisible and impenetrable shield.

The boy's own life experiences continue to detract from his self-esteem. The failures begin to multiply. Difficulties at school, the second most significant environment for children, are universal for this population. Often, simple and straightforward interventions such as pharmacological treatment for those with attention-deficit hyperactivity disorders, which could have provided relief or accelerated behavior change, were not tried, or were not even available. The message is clear and painful to them. Success is not to be expected outside of the home either. They are labeled by social institutions, and self-fulfilling prophecies reach fruition.

As identified above, the predominant emotional issue with which these boys cope is abysmally low self-worth. The causes of the lowered self-esteem are numerous. Racially, they are part of a disenfranchised minority that has yet to achieve political and social power in proportion to its numbers. Culturally, they are typically very poor, and perhaps most vulnerable to the messages of an affluent majority that communicate that successful and worthwhile life equals the continual acquisition of more expensive "things." The constant commercial bombardment from the media of our consuming society reminds them of their low place in society and contributes to their alienation from the rest of "us." These issues further complicate the complexity of their lives.

When all of these factors come together, the results are often lethal. The youth has an underdeveloped conscience, and low self-esteem. He is enraged, rejected, and ashamed, unable to temporally or morally comprehend the consequences of and take responsibility for his behavior. He emerges with no fear of social punishment. Even the death penalty will not deter him, because he is partially dead already. In a way, his survival strengthens his adolescent sense of invulnerability and reinforces his natural competence. These adolescents minimize society's threats as unreal, and at the same time overreact to the threat of someone on the street. They are fatalists and will often verbalize that "hey, everybody's got to go." This is further evidence of their massive denial.

Closely related is Wurmser's (1981) conceptualization of shamelessness. Feeling profoundly humiliated by his life experiences, the adolescent defends against its conscious recognition by the defense mechanism of reversal. Unable to accept his own weaknesses, the youth copes by inverting his self-contempt, directing it outward. He behaves as if he has no values. His shamelessness is shocking and appears almost subhuman. We see the dynamics in the following example.

> Jerome was a 15-year-old incarcerated for possessing a pistol. He had a quiet demeanor, and was usually overlooked by staff, except when they become annoyed by his icy glares in response to one of their requests. He had lived with his aunt for the past several years. His mother refused to take responsibility for him. He reported that his mother was a recovering alcoholic who just gave birth to another son. Jerome's father has been in and out of jail for most of his life. He had been

incarcerated for the past five years, with several more years to serve. Jerome stated that he did not know the crime for which his father was convicted. Jerome first became known to the courts as a toddler. His mother physically abused and neglected him, and was unable to provide adequate shelter for him as they moved from place to place. His records report placement at six different elementary schools. Finally, he was taken away from his mother and placed in foster care, eventually ending up with his aunt.

His peer group consists of older, paternalistic teenagers whom he described as enforcers and contract killers. Jerome himself was once shot four times and left for dead. Jerome continually fantasized about the reconstitution of his nuclear family. This was impossible because of the incarceration of his father, the unwillingness of a younger sister to even speak to her mother, a 3-year-old brother in foster care, and the mother's new son by another man.

Jerome was a demanding and whiny boy, never able to get enough attention from staff. His rage appeared limitless. A resident once made the mistake of challenging him to a fight. Though Jerome says that he tried to avoid the altercation, the other boy would be not be dissuaded, so Jerome took the challenge. The boy's eye was the size of a tennis ball after Jerome's punches. When told about the punishment for punching the other boy, he shrugged his shoulders. "So what? *You* can't do anything to hurt me," he responded.

Jerome's rage is at least as scary to him. He once discussed the mutilation of a troublesome crime victim with a mixture of shock and repulsion, describing his own behavior as "treacherous." It seemed that an addict whom a drug dealing friend of Jerome's supplied became desperate enough to steal from this friend. Upon learning of the robbery, Jerome and his friends sought the addict out. First, he was beaten about the head with a lead pipe. As he lay on the ground, Jerome proceeded to chop off his two middle fingers with a meat cleaver. He related the story dispassionately, without the boyish braggadocio so frequently seen in the population.

The anger of some of these abandoned and unloved adolescents knows no bounds. The same boy who is capable of sweetness and tenderness toward his sister and friends, can respond with murderous rage in the blink of an eye, much like the soldier who massacres "enemies" even as he carries photos of his similar loved ones in his breast pocket.

DRUG USAGE

With regard to substance abuse, two divergent patterns emerge. While most of the youngsters do not use drugs, some turn to substance abuse to cope with the pain of their experiences and the subsequent shame and rage. Those boys who fear the effects of the drugs or find them dysphoric abstain.

Non-users

One of the more important trends noted by many workers in the local criminal justice system is the decreased prevalence of drug usage by those arrested, especially those arrested for selling drugs. Using young boys to transport and sell drugs is a well-known strategy of older dealers, since the local juvenile justice system is renowned for its inconsistent and light sentences. In general, a 2-year commitment means a 6- to 8-month incarceration in an overburdened system. In addition, the children are bamboozled by their young adult bosses who minimize the significance and discomfort of the juvenile detention facility.

According to the adolescents, there is a general understanding among most of those who sell drugs: "Usage is not permitted." Apparently, the older "lieutenants" recognize that a soldier who uses makes an unreliable dealer, consuming and/or losing expensive merchandise. What occurs, for all intents and purposes, is pre-employment screening, where reliable sources, namely other dealers, are queried as to the veracity of the "applicants'" statements. Only after his sobriety is established is he hired.

The reasons for selling drugs ("hustling") vary, but generally involve making of large sums of money quickly. Some of the money is used to support the family. Most of it is spent on designer clothing, jewelry, and automobiles that increase their popularity with their peers, especially girls. This bolsters self-esteem. After all, if they own what society tells them they should, they finally achieve some social value. Many of these boys sell drugs, but only a smaller number use. Even that usage appears to be irregular. Court-mandated urine tests at arrest support this.

Substance Abusers

Those who use drugs usually begin to take them as a way to combat boredom. The drugs end up being used as an anesthetic. As with the American soldiers in Vietnam, substance abuse allows them to forget the horror of yesterday, and to avoid focusing upon the potentially cataclysmic events of tomorrow. Before 1985, Phencyclidine (PCP) was the drug of choice among this population. Since then, it has been supplanted by crack cocaine. Marijuana is also used by many, but its use appears to be becoming increasingly sporadic.

Significant levels of substance abuse are reported amongst the young adults with whom the residents associate. One possible explanation might be related to the life situation of the young black male 15-year-old versus a black male 25-year-old. By age 25, they begin to have a better understanding about what social and economic possibilities are and are not available. Such an understanding may lead to depression and rage. This in turn leads to more regular substance abuse to cope with cultural anomie (Durkheim, 1897/1951) and disenfranchisement. The discrepancy between what they have been led to believe is possible, and what in reality is attainable, becomes all too apparent.

TRANSFERENCE AND RESISTANCE ISSUES

On an individual level, as stated above, most of these youth have been "abandoned" by their biological fathers through divorce, separation, substance abuse, incarceration, murder, and so on. It matters little if this abandonment was volitional, imposed by the criminal justice system, or a matter of fate. The net result is the same. Some have experienced similar rejections from their biological mothers, with even more dramatic impact. Many have been victims of child abuse and neglect, usually physical abuse but frequently sexual. The main result is a person who feels dirty, used, weak, stupid, abandoned, rejected, unloved, and inadequate — in a word, worthless. Their best natural defense and logical consequence to their life circumstances is rage. Getting an adolescent to discuss these issues is very problematic, because of the rage, the strong social taboo against talking about themselves and their feelings, and normal psychological defenses, especially denial. For those who have been sexually abused, there seems to be a particularly strong taboo among black adolescents about the admission of homosexual acts perpetrated upon them.

To do therapy with them, you must constantly remember that these boys are creatures of shame. They are immersed in it. It is woven into the fabric of their being (cf., Nathanson, 1987; Wurmser, 1981). To that end, it is important to interpret their transference-related behaviors in therapy such as silence, verbal aggression, and walking out of the room as related to shame. They are designed to protect the integrity of the individual, to avoid embarrassment and humiliation, and to keep others at arm's length. So long as the psychotherapist is at arm's length, he or she will not discover what the child already knows, namely, in his most intimate sense of himself he is inadequate, weak, unlovable, and worthless. To reveal himself, to demonstrate before others his shortcomings, to be seen as unlovable, he runs the risk of yet another rejection, with subsequent abandonment. As this has occurred frequently throughout his life and in many different forms, he is consciously and unconsciously organized to avoid such events at all costs, even if it means losing the benefits of closeness that intimacy with other human beings brings. This is reflected in the different types of resistances encountered in therapy. These adolescents do not know *how* to attach to another human being in a loving, intimate, and respectful way.

The most typical resistance used in psychotherapy by these boys is a passive stance that denies that any kind of feelings or thoughts are occurring at all. All inquiries about feelings are met with denial. They are estranged from their emotions and depersonalize their whole experience (Wurmser, 1981). This can best be responded to by acceptance at the outset. However, as these youngsters can be infinitely stoic, capable of avoiding issues forever, eventually the therapist must confront them. Usually, you begin a confrontation by obtaining information from other sources such as his parent, social worker, or cottage counselor. Questions and concerns about this information are best presented in a curious, nonaccusatory manner, rather than unexpectedly exclaiming that a particular issue must be a problem to him.

Finally, these adolescents, typically being from dysfunctional families whether or not substance abuse per se is occurring by them or in their families, demonstrate the same kind of resistance behaviors as those who were raised in substance abusing families. They experienced inconsistency and chaos, a lack of acknowledgment of feelings, proscriptions against talking, a lack of trust, neglect, uncontrolled rage, and so forth. As a result, these children adopt the same roles such as the loner, the family hero, and the problem child. They follow the same rules of behavior such as not trusting others, not feeling bad emotions, and so on, outlined by Black (1981) and Wood (1987). Avoidance, aggressiveness, assaultiveness, and passivity are all manifestations of the issues that these adolescents take to the battlefield of the streets and bring to the psychotherapist's office serving in the psychological MASH unit.

These unconscious transference behaviors are simultaneously designed to keep the adolescent safe and the psychotherapist at a distance. They have allowed the adolescent to survive under the most difficult conditions short of a major war. Therefore, it is incumbent upon those working with this population to respect their presence. When that does not occur, the youngster will sense it, and begin to act out in self-punishing and self-destructive ways. As this happens, the psychotherapist must begin to examine the type of countertransference reaction he is undergoing to get the helping process back on track.

COUNTERTRANSFERENCE ISSUES

Countertransference issues abound for the psychotherapist working in a juvenile detention setting. Coping with residents and staff that behave in a stereotyped, self-destructive manner while manag-

ing to elicit your own similar and repressed feelings and thoughts
are what make fighting the war so difficult on an individual level.
Acknowledging their existence and monitoring their effects are the
only ways to make success more likely.

Anger

Dealing with these issues begins with the recognition that the first
feeling you experience is your anger. Most of these children are
absolute masters at eliciting anger from those with whom they interact. They are quite uncomfortable when they find themselves with
an adult who is not angry and punishing. It is unfamiliar territory.
They unconsciously act in a manner to ensure that you will become
openly hostile. This is done in diverse ways, ranging from aggressive invasions of your personal space to withholding by sitting in
stony silence during sessions.

It is important that your anger not be expressed through hostile
verbal comments or the kind of arguments that frequently occur
between staff and residents. To avoid these, you must move away
from the situations as they become overwhelming. Often, colleagues become useful outlets with whom you can acceptably vent
your anger and frustration without endangering the therapeutic relationship with the boy. Time away can create some emotional distance, allowing you to understand it for the transference behavior
that it is. This makes it less likely to feel personally attacked, less-
ening the probability that you will respond in kind.

Inadequacy and Shame

Feelings of inadequacy and ineffectiveness are also experienced
frequently. Typical expectations about client behavior must be sus-
pended, or else you will begin to question your most basic compe-
tencies as a psychotherapist. The conditions of treatment, including
the setting and the life experiences of the youngsters, are so different than those of traditional psychotherapy clients that you may
conclude that they make working toward positive therapeutic goals
impossible.

Another way that the adolescents defend against their feelings of
inadequacy and shame is to project them onto you. Suddenly, you

become impotent, unable to effectively intervene to help this boy feel better. All efforts at intervention are unconsciously thwarted by the youth. Your own anger and frustration about the boy's inability to behave more appropriately are indicators of such projection. Feelings of shame about your lack of effectiveness can occur through projective identification, when the boy refuses to acknowledge or own his feelings of shame, instead evoking those feelings within the psychotherapist.

This can be best dealt with through consultation with colleagues. Their input will enable you to become aware of previously unconsidered techniques, or assure that you are doing all that can be done, helping to modify your expectations, and subsequent negative valuations.

Setting

Extra-therapist factors, such as the physical setting, or the disdainful treatment of the importance of the psychotherapy sessions by the staff, can be so problematic that despite recognizing it, such factors can still influence psychotherapy. Such hindrances can lead you to become overinvolved with the boy and his treatment at the facility, focusing too much on how line staff responds to the patient's needs and behaviors. What can develop is an "us versus them" perspective, where staff behaviors become interpreted as sabotaging the daily functioning of the child, or the therapeutic relationship.

This can be seductive from the standpoint of solidifying the therapeutic alliance by uniting against a common enemy (cf. Sherif, Harvey, White, Hood, & Sherif, 1961). It can also be destructive by leading to a reduction in necessary confrontation. The youth's inappropriate thoughts or behaviors can be excused or avoided, because of the treatment that the boy is currently receiving from staff, or because of his traumatic past. Anger at the staff is an indicator that this is occurring, as well as the fantasy is that no one can quite understand him as well as you.

Another example of these overinvolvement or overprotection effects involves taking the boy beyond the bounds of the traditional psychotherapy relationship for a "novel therapeutic experience."

For example, moving a youngster off-grounds, or taking him home for the weekend has occurred as a sympathetic response to the boy who does not have the level of family involvement of other residents, such as telephone calls or weekend visitors. While meant well, this will confuse the youngster as to the boundaries of the relationship. An interesting aspect to these overprotective countertransference phenomena is that line staff seem to have an innate, unconscious ability to perceive the existence of this type of relationship. Their response is usually swift and exact. They "discriminate" against the adolescent in the form of negative reinforcements and punishments for the slightest wrong. This is an important self-correcting mechanism that can enable you to interpret your anger at staff as a signal that you are overprotecting the patient. At that time, you need to critically examine your behaviors. Future special treatment or extra involvement with the boy should be avoided.

Silence

As mentioned above, a silent therapy session with an adolescent is a frequent occurrence. Unimportant questions and issues may be responded to, but salient concerns will be avoided by silence. In addition to anger, another countertransference response may be to terminate the session as well as future contacts with the boy. Since so many residents are unserved, little justification is needed to move to another boy who appears so much more attractive because of his willingness to hold a dialogue. Acceptance of the silent anger of some boys and perseverance on the part of the psychotherapist is necessary for the adolescent intent on replicating such a rejection scenario in treatment.

Confusion

Finally, many of these youths are particularly skilled at providing excuses for inappropriate behaviors. Often, these excuses are offered in such a cognitively disordered manner that only sensitivity to such a defensive maneuver will enable you to confront it. Your confusion will act as an indicator that this may be occurring. This presentation can be the product of his denial, in the narrower forms of rationalization, minimization, or projection. It may also be a manipulation. If so, it needs to be confronted directly. You must not become just one more adult that the boy has put one over on. In addition, when you demonstrate your understanding that you have been manipulated, it is not the same thing as becoming angry at the attempt. If anger is aroused, you can appropriately model that it does not lead to aggression or rejection. Let's explore this in the following example.

Robert is a 17 year-old youth who was arrested for possession of cocaine with intent to distribute. Originally from Jamaica, he came to America with his older brother and mother when he was six. He lives out of state. He and many others bring drugs to our city, where they can be sold for more money. He left home several years ago after quarreling with his mother, and lived on the streets. He had not spoken to her since their last encounter, when he became so enraged that he chased her around her apartment with a carving knife. At present, Robert's older brother is an engineer, employed by the Army, and married. His success and attractiveness were often used as an example by his mother of what Robert was not.

Robert's adjustment at the facility was difficult. He engaged in numerous fist fights in his maximum-security unit. They were usually initiated by the taunting of his nationality and out-of-state residence by the other boys. This resulted in his being punished frequently. He had a paranoid-like perspective of the other residents and staff, believing them to be out to hurt him and make his life miserable.

At the outset of treatment, he was extremely resistant to the idea that his actions were defensive responses to others' attacks on his nationality. In classic reaction formation, Robert declared himself proud of his heritage. By confronting him about the reasons for his pugilistic responses to their gibes, the psychotherapist was gradually able to help him understand and acknowledge that their comments were injurious to his self-esteem and, feeling ashamed, he defended with rage.

As psychotherapy progressed, he tested the therapist in a number of ways. He refused to acknowledge any responsibility for the altercations, dismissing them as the inevitable consequence of incarceration with criminals. "This is a jail," he informed the psychotherapist. During one session, he demanded to know whether the psychotherapist thought him "crazy." He would not be assuaged by the response. The result was an angry tantrum that did not feel authentic to the psychotherapist.

The psychotherapist responded by interpreting the concern as a self-esteem and shame-related issue, much like the fist fights which had been previously discussed. The interpretation now seemed plausible, and he settled down. This response, and the lack of an angry retort from the attacked psychotherapist, were the major solidifying factors in the therapeutic alliance. Robert was later able to admit that he realized that he was testing the psychotherapist, and that this was his way to discern trustworthiness.

A manipulative boy, Robert attempted to use the psychotherapist to obtain a minimum-security placement and eventual weekend visits from the facility. The psychotherapist agreed to advocate for him if behavioral changes occurred.

The fist fights ceased over the course of the next several weeks. An articulate and introspective youngster, he was able by the conclusion of treatment to recognize, label, and interpret his own problem behaviors as resulting from injuries to his own self-esteem and the consequent anger. He was especially thoughtful about his last run-in with his mother, and eventually telephoned her. They reached some type of truce and returned to speaking terms before he was transferred from the facility. Robert's future plans included an out-of-state move to live with his brother and his wife.

Even as you acknowledge your feelings and monitor their presence, you will probably feel overwhelmed by the odds that you face. At times, no matter how effective and well timed the intervention, the results will underwhelm both the youth and the staff. These outcomes and sometimes the job in general can be best coped with by limiting expectations of change and definitions of successful outcomes. Like a never-ending bloody battle of attrition, the war goes on. The names change, but the faces and the wounds do not. Any respite proves temporary in a MASH unit.

CONCLUSIONS

Providing services to the largely poor, black, male population of a juvenile detention facility is filled with problems. However, it is never boring. These adolescents are truly those Missing In Action, the forgotten soldiers, in our current battle-torn culture. Of those that physically survive, most will go on to become tomorrow's adult criminal offenders, filling adult prisons in the 1990s as so many of their fathers do today. We collude to forget them. The scarcity of professional literature about them and the inadequate services provided for them is both frustrating and telling. Because youth from multiproblem families are the most likely to suffer the most extensive physical abuse and neglect (Watters, White, Parry, Caplan, & Bates, 1986), and are least likely to receive help for financial and cultural reasons, we can conclude that they will not go away. Most will continue to be our "social problems" for their entire lives. Some have already begun to father the next generation of street soldiers.

Some longitudinal data suggests that their futures may not be as bleak as we suppose (Long & Vaillant, 1984). Some studies offer empirical guidelines for intervention with similar populations (cited in Werry & Wollersheim, 1989). Most professionals in the field seem to share the belief that successful outcomes when working with these boys are rare, especially when drug abuse is involved (Cancrini, Cingolani, Compagnoni, Constantini, & Mazzoni, 1988).

What is clear is that the war continues, spurred on by the social and cultural factors of poverty and drugs. Though practitioners on the front lines usually do not have the luxury of writing about or scientifically studying what it is that we do, because of limited resources, it is important for us to recognize that this is what we must do. The lack of data and clinical observation may be a large part of why we are so impotent today in terms of affecting change. Though it may not be as pressing as the immediate crisis on which we are focused, it is only through such research and discourse that ideas are shared and scientific progress occurs. These are the activities which we must perform if we are to ultimately help to alleviate some of the burden which these adolescents have been forced to carry in order to bring the war to an end for some of them.

REFERENCES

Bauer, G. P., & Kobos, J. C. (1987). *Brief therapy: Short-term psychodynamic intervention*. Northvale, NJ: Aronson.

Black, C. (1981). *It will never happen to me!* Denver: M.A.C.

Cancrini, L., Cingolani S., Compagnoni, F., Constantini, D., & Mazzoni, S. (1988). Juvenile drug addiction: A typology of heroin addicts and their families. *Family Process, 27*, 261-271.

Dash, L. (1989). *When children want children: Urban crisis of childbearing*. New York: Morrow.

Durkheim, E. (1951). *Le suicide* (Suicide). New York: Free Press. (Original work published in 1897)

Jourard, S. M. (1964). *The transparent self*. Princeton, NJ: D. Van Nostrand.

Kohut, H. (1979). The two analyses of Mr. Z. *International Journal of Psychoanalysis, 60*, 3-27.

Long, J. V. F., & Vaillant, G. E. (1984). Natural history of male psychological health, XI: Escape from the underclass. *American Journal of Psychiatry, 141*, 341-346.

Marmor, J. (1979). Short-term dynamic psychotherapy. *American Journal of Psychiatry, 136*, 149-155.

Maslow, A. H. (1968). *Toward a psychology of being* (2nd ed.). Princeton, NJ: D. Van Nostrand.

Nathanson, D. L. (Ed.). (1987). *The many faces of shame*. New York: Guilford.

Sherif, M., Harvey, O. J., White, B. J., Hood, W., & Sherif, C. (1961). *Intergroup conflict and cooperation: The robber's cave experiment*. Norman, OK: University of Oklahoma (Institute of Intergroup Relations).

Watters, J., White, G., Parry, R., Caplan, P., & Bates, R. (1986). A comparison of child abuse and neglect. *Canadian Journal of Behavioral Science, 18*, 449-459.

Werry. J. S., & Wollersheim, J. P. Behavior therapy with children and adolescents: A twenty year overview. *Journal of the American Academy of Child and Adolescent Psychiatry, 28*, 1-18.

Wood, B. (1987). *Children of alcoholism*. New York: New York University Press.

Wurmser, L. (1981). *The mask of shame*. Baltimore: The Johns Hopkins University Press.

A Presence Among the Poor:
An Interview
with Brother Robert (Bob) Lombardo, MS

E. Mark Stern, Interviewer

SUMMARY. An interview with a Franciscan friar working as a pastoral counselor and administrator of a small shelter for homeless men in New York City. The interview focuses on the several types of poverty: economic, intellectual, psychological and spiritual. Brother Bob emphasizes a pastoral vantage point in working with those who are poor and homeless.

Brother Bob: I am a Franciscan friar working in a men's shelter in the South Bronx. At the beginning of his conversion almost 800 years ago, Saint Francis embraced a leper and began to care for those afflicted with that horrible disease. Following the inspiration and example of Saint Francis, the Franciscans over the centuries have chosen to care for the very poor outcasts of society. In our attempt to faithfully follow Saint Francis, the newly established Franciscan Friars of the Renewal have chosen to work with the very poor in our society. After many months of hard work renovating the old Saint Adalbert's Convent, the Friars have opened the Padre Pio Shelter on December 23, 1987. Because the convent building was not suited for a shelter and because our new community of sisters

Brother Robert (Bob) Lombardo was at the time of this interview a graduate student at the Graduate Division of Pastoral and Family Counseling at Iona College in New Rochelle, NY. He is a vowed member of the Franciscan Friars of the Renewal. Mailing Address: Saint Crispin Friary, 420 East 156 St., Bronx, NY 10455.

Dr. Stern, Editor of *The Psychotherapy Patient* is the interviewer. Mailing address: 215 East 11 St., New York, NY 10003

133

was forming and would need the convent, we began to make plans to relocate the shelter. The Roman Catholic Archdiocese of New York gave us a large unused section of Saint Adalbert's School as the new home for the shelter. This unused section of the school was in a state of disrepair and needed extensive renovations. The renovations began in June of 1989. We try to keep it small in order to keep an intimacy by avoiding turning people into numbers. After all, being homeless has meant being without a home — no one knowing your name. It's easy for me to understand the notion of numbers since before entering religious life I worked as an accountant.

E. Mark Stern: How did you arrive at your current place in life? After all, as a religious you take a vow of poverty, in addition to vows of chastity and obedience.

Br. B: When I was a college student, a fellow student died of spinal meningitis. I happened to be there at the very end. It led me to question the purpose of my own life. I was impressed with the priests on campus who so ably helped us deal with the death of someone so young. Eventually I became associated with Franscican life. We emphasize two major works in our community. One is with the poor and especially the homeless. The other dimension is preaching the Catholic faith.

EMS: You've also been in graduate training at Iona College in pastoral counseling. How does this flavor your approach to your apostolate?

Br. B: It is very easy to give someone a sandwich or make a bed, or even clean out a bathroom. But counseling with the homeless is a major challenge. I've had to learn about myself in order to be more helpful with people. As a vowed religious, who incidentally wears a Franscican habit, I have found that my role makes it much easier for people to unburden themselves. And as I listen, it becomes clear how a person's conception of God has a bearing on self-regard.

EMS: Are you suggesting that this involves seeing their own poverty as the outcome of sin?

Br. B: I don't see this as a necessary connection, though it's sometimes a complicating concern as to where the person has finally arrived. Important in counseling is where the person came from. But poverty wears many faces. There is a poverty of the have-nots — poor housing conditions, not nearly enough food. Then there is an intellectual poverty. This occurs where there have been few educational opportunities and where education has not been valued. Whatever intellectual capacities may be there have simply not been developed. Then of course there is the most unfortunate psychological poverty. Here the person has been blighted with low self-esteem, often due to the an unsupportive and uncaring family system. This results in a poor and destructive way of relating resulting in major emotional disadvantages. Finally there is a poverty which I recognize here in New York which I didn't experience in my mission work in Bolivia. There they are economically poorer than even the poorest of neighborhoods in this city. But here there is a deeper poverty, a condition I understand as a spiritual lack. With some type of relationship with God, the most blatant of economic deprivations is viewed in a different context. Belief in a higher force enables a person to deal with poverty more constructively.

EMS: I gather that you have a dedication to the Franciscan concept of Lady Poverty. Here the most humbled of existences interact in a meaningful whole.

Br. B: Lady Poverty was much loved by Saint Francis. This love remains a key ingredient in Franciscan life. Francis envisioned an emphasis on God's gifts as contrasted with those of the material world. Creation as such is beautiful, but it is merely a mirror of the Creator. So "things" in themselves don't become an end. Their worth is seen as a gateway to the divine plan. This speaks to a society geared to a materialistic be-all and end-all. Note however that Lady Poverty doesn't mean deprivation of a personhood. Instead, she speaks to a prioritizing of those things and values which have importance to the individual's journey through life.

EMS: There is an old Shaker hymn which speaks of the gift to be simple. It is this giftedness which endows a person with much spiritual wealth.

Br. B: I see that gift as putting life within a perspective. There are perhaps the same number of needs. The core to the gift is how and in what manner we satisfy them. God as a focus or priority allows other needs to fall into an appropriate place. For example, does one need a coat for each and every occasion, or is it possible that values other than acquisition allow the person to be satisfied with what is essential to make it through the winter? There is a way of seeing material goods for what they are, but not looking to them to be more than they are.

EMS: How does your Franciscan frame of reference make your counseling approach viable with the poor: those who are materially poor and those who are spiritually impoverished?

Br. B: I think that my priorities might differ from the more specifically secular counseling encounters. I would tend to place much less emphasis on the quest for material goods as a means to happiness or fulfillment. I would underline the several modes of relationship to self, to others, and to God. This in no way downplays the terrible fate of material poverty. Much has to be done to eradicate the injustices which underlie hunger, homelessness and, illiteracy.

EMS: I guess it's safe to say that your concerns are bi-modal. On the one hand you deal with poverty as a blight on society, while on the other hand you strive for the meaning within what poverty has to offer.

Br. B: That's basically accurate. My interest is in prioritizing loss and gain. There is still one more aspect to my work. I try to motivate people out of the situation of material and psychological poverty. You could say that my goal is to help provide the necessary hope to make this a possibility. I think education, job opportunities, better housing are fundamental. And while we're at it, it becomes necessary to help the individual to come to terms with the interpersonal conflicts which destroy any real measure of hope. Despair is, after all, the dissembler of hope. I think that, with all good intentions, there have been people who, in their attempts to help the poor and disenfranchised, instilled a sense of anger in them. This somehow may have injured the motivations to do better with their lives.

EMS: I gather then that your work is at its base transformational. You underscore the need for a sense of inner worth and spiritual wholeness.

Br. B: An example comes to mind. A young man came to our shelter. He had had a bad situation with his wife and was literally thrown out of his house because of both abusing and dealing drugs. Obviously his wife had become fearful on many levels. She feared retaliation from people in the drug-dealing world. He had certainly acknowledged the severe crisis he had been going through and now wanted very much to get back with his family. He did go through detoxification and wanted to follow through on what you might term the "straight and narrow." He remained in the shelter for a time, and while there woke up one morning feeling quite physically ill. His glands were swollen and his throat ached. The doctor diagnosed him as having lymphoma. Further tests confirmed that he had AIDS. From all that he said, I was the only person he felt confident in talking to regarding his fears of the eventual outcome of his illness. He was deeply saddened by the prospect of never seeing his wife and children again. Coupled with this was his terror of dying. The confrontation with death had been like running head on into a brick wall. Of course my counseling training was essential. It helped me ferret out my own fears so that I could better deal with his issues.

EMS: It's obvious that your role in the neighborhood elicits confidence. You bring a special quality to your work. From your vantage point, what do you see as important for the secular counselor working with the impoverished?

Br. B: Being willing to bear with the person, to truly listen. This is the means through which one can get beyond the sad stereotyping that's done with the poor and homeless. Such stereotypes include "the crazy person" or "the skid-row bum" and so forth. It's essential to go beyond such tempting typologies and learn to reach the human soul that is actually there. One can't even attempt such reaching unless there is an acceptance of the person where he or she is at. No matter what the commonalities among the poor—addiction, economic disadvantage, or even a physical handicap—they are souls coming from some place and attempting to arrive somewhere.

EMS: It's obviously no easy matter for the person to get beyond his or her own stereotypes. Stereotypes must serve the person in some manner or other?

Br. B: Sure. Stereotypes are often a person's only defense against the hurts and tragedies in their backgrounds. It's here that the self-stereotyping can serve to keep others at a safe distance from these hurts. Hurts are, after all, signs of vulnerability. People who come into the shelter are frequently defensive and self-protective. Some won't even take their coats off. Yet once they begin to feel some security where they are, a slow process emerges. They visibly become more available by allowing someone else to get beyond their self-styled boundaries. Ultimately, it's the person's isolation which is the real challenge. But one can't limit stereotypes to the underclassed. I too am looked at stereotypically. Just looking at me enwrapped in my religious garb may make a person quite defensive in regard to their network of sinful behaviors. I'm not afraid of this stereotype since I do believe firmly in what the Church teaches. As a result, I do understand that I can't help everyone. Certainly my stereotype can lead to another level of dialogue between me and the other person. I may open up concerns about God's wrath. These are legitimate fears people may have to deal with as they confront their own destinies. The young man I referred to earlier who had been diagnosed with AIDS did worry about his stake in guilt and its consequences regarding his salvation. Here I was able to use the stereotype of the religious person constructively, to speak of God's love and mercy.

EMS: It's fascinating to think of what happens when two stereotypes actually meet. Does it happen that when they reach the essence of what the stereotypes represent that they might evoke some profound communication? Becomes, as it were, sacred encounter?

Br. B: A premise we Franciscans have is that each person is created in God's image and likeness. So as Jesus said, "Whatsoever you do to the least little one, you do unto me." I'm not claiming to always be conscious of that divine claim. There are times I'm tempted to wring someone's neck. But down where it counts, I believe in the basic worth of the individual soul. There is some element of God in each personality.

EMS: So despite all conscious resistances to it, the wellspring of the person made in God's image becomes a fundamental construct in your counseling. Perhaps this awareness may only happen through a rear-view mirror, but it happens nonetheless. It is, as it were, the uncommon denominator of your work.

Br. B: One major aspect of this is the frequent request for my prayers on their behalf. People I have most successfully dealt with do believe in the power of such intercessory prayer. Each morning before leaving the shelter, we say a little prayer asking God to protect those entrusted to us throughout their day. Regardless of other preoccupations, these men ask for our daily prayers. This becomes an aspect of the empowerment of surviving some very difficult circumstances. I'd like to see more counselors become aware of the foundational effectiveness of prayer. I'd never want to force a person into my spiritual position. I just want to make them aware of this availability in me.

EMS: Calling upon a divine presence to be experienced, even celebrated, becomes a vital function of your counseling. So even when there is an inner paucity or lack of real belief in the person, just the calling out for help becomes prayer in itself. In that connection, I recall reading that when Thomas Merton was being eulogized by the then Archabbot, and currently Archbishop Weakland, it was stated that the ideal of the novice contemplative was to seek God in all ways, even if he found no clear evidence of the Creator in his consciousness. So it is in the cry for help that the real journey begins and proceeds.

Br. B: It is just this which operates: God hasn't appeared to help in a person's life struggles. So the question begins to arise as to one's personal worthiness. All the more need for spiritual guidance and direction in order to help a person go beyond the misconceptions of a vengeful God.

EMS: I hear throughout our discussion that authentic listening is a way of keeping faith. And here is the hope. It's your ability to keep in touch with the creaturehood of the poor and disadvantaged that operates as a healing presence. This goes a distance beyond mere reassurance. Such reassurance rarely blossoms into positive results in working with the downtrodden.

Br. B: I'm glad that you brought that up since one of the main differences I see between my working in a shelter and being in a strictly counseling situation is that I'm there on a day-to-day basis. I interact with the men on many diverging levels. I'm not only counselor, but I'm also there as cook and homemaker. As I reflect on this family-type atmosphere, it leads me to the conclusion that being part and parcel of a support system is basic to my mission with the residents of the shelter. We are currently negotiating with the State in eventually setting up a more permanent living facility. This does entail bringing a new family to birth—with all that such a coming into being entails, the good and the bad. The purpose would be to deal with the family in a constructive, and not in a destructive manner. Even in the present shelter, which offers only limited care, we do what might significantly be termed family therapy.

EMS: And as authentic family therapy, it becomes an evolutionary process. In a family, the hope is that there is movement from infantile helplessness to a generative place in the world. Borrowing from Saint Augustine, the project becomes a step toward establishing the city of God — in this case the family of God.

Br. B: We presently have role supervisors. Our hope is that they can help establish the appropriateness of community in the lives of the homeless men we serve. The idea is to help instill a sense of responsibility which can be made to work in all of their settings. With responsibility there's less the danger of imposing another form of poverty — the poverty of helplessness and ineffectiveness. Together with many volunteers, the Friars and Sisters attempt to provide a safe, clean, and homelike atmosphere for the shelter guests. As I alluded to earlier, looking into the future, we hope to open up an additional residence for the homeless to be named after Saint Anthony. This residence will be located in what is now a six-floor abandoned tenement. When finally renovated, the new residence will house 65 men. The Friars and Sisters require generous support from the public to continue our work and to assist with construction costs. Should any reader choose to help us as a benefactor, that would certainly be appreciated. Checks should be made out to Padre Pio Shelter, c/o Saint Crispin Friary, 420 East 156 Street, Bronx, New York 10455.

EMS: It's been a pleasure to have this time with you. I know that your work and your personal insights into the many forms of poverty will be of major help to the practicing psychotherapist. Many of our impressions of the homeless are second or third hand. We do know that the many tracts of poverty have a deep impact on us all. Your work broadens our work. Thank you for your special form of perseverance.

Poverty:
A Vision for Heterotopic Eyes,
A Question of Values

Kris Jeter

SUMMARY. The challenge to professionals working with the poor is the active choice and display of values. The therapist is challenged to avoid imposing individual values on others to promote conformity, and to immobilize personal values in order not to influence others. There is a need to expand our consciousness regarding poverty from our own clientele to all of humankind. An addition to Maslow's theory of the hierarchy of needs is proposed.

Once upon a time there was a 9-year old girl who moved from a prairie town of entrepreneurs to a mountain village of coal miners whose coal was no longer desired. Their young adults moved to the big cities. The folks who remained wore the band-aids of welfare dollars. During the girl's education in the elementary school, she gave her two-cent milk to a classmate—pregnant by her own father. With her young mind, she remembered the paradise of her past

Kris Jeter, PhD, is Associate Director of Mentor and Learner Relationships for the Human Capacities Training Program and Director of Programs and Communications for The Possible Society. Dr. Jeter is the Analytic Essay Editor for the international journal, *Marriage and Family Review.* She is the author of over 50 publications and the producer of over 40 photo essays and illustrated lectures. Her scholarly work is on the family over the life cycle; utilizing the family as a unit of analysis in research; and examining its important linkages and interactions with larger bureaucratic organizations. Dr. Jeter incorporates in her work international anthropology, archaeology, art, history, literature, mythology, religion, sociology, and psychology. She is interested in the programming, facilitation, and evaluation of the affective, cognitive, and psychomotor learning processes using various techniques. Mailing address: 800 Paper Mill Road, Newark, DE 19711.

*where the milk flowed for everyone and childhood was childhood
unlayered with parenthood.*

This story is true and is my own. It changed the course of my life.
I devoted my life to the education and civil rights of people of all
economic statuses. I anticipate that all professionals who work with
the financially impoverished have a story in their past that influenced their choice of a career.

A person learns values, the placement of resources of energy,
money, and time, from infancy within the family unit. It is part of
the family coding. As a person is trained, the values of the institution, built not around service but around the preeminence of the
profession, most often occur. The professional knows best. Unless
a professional probes deeply into her or his conscious and unconscious, it is doubtful if there will be a radical transformation of
values. Permanent shifts in behavior and values occur because a
person believes profoundly that change is both possible and necessary.

One of the major challenges that faces the professional who
works with the poor is the active choice and display of values. The
therapist's values affect the client's values and reciprocation occurs. The therapist faces the challenge of placing her or his style on
a continuum from imposing individual values on others for the promotion of conformity, to immobilizing personal values so that others are not influenced.

*Once upon a time there were three brothers of a poor, rural
family, age five, six, and seven, who were playing ball near an
irrigation ditch. With the spring rains, the ditch had become quite
deep. Trying to catch one ball, the 7-year-old boy slipped into the
ditch. The 6-year-old boy jumped into the ditch to save his brother,
gasping for air, and he also began to flail, gasp, and sink. The 5-
year-old boy remembered the words of his kindergarten teacher,
"Never go into water to save anyone. Get help." He ran to his
home and told his mother. His mother picked up the telephone and
found the 16-line party line engaged. She begged to have the line to
phone the police. She was denied access to the line. The two boys
died.*

A co-owner of the local small-market radio station went to visit the members of the surviving family. The mother freely told her the story and it was tastefully reported to the community. The news story was picked up by the national news services. People and corporations from all over the United States empathized with the unnecessary loss and donated money to the family. Ford Motor Company paid off the remaining payments for the family pickup truck so that the family could start life again with debt-free transportation. Imagine the surprise of the members of the local charity effort led by the county welfare department's social worker, all drivers of cars 5 years and older, to learn that the father immediately went to the local Ford car dealership and traded his year old pickup for the newest model.

The above story is true. My mother was the news reporter. The well-meaning social worker and members of the local charity effort faced a clash of values. Stories about the differences in the appropriation of resources similar to this story abound and often initiate the professional's reconsideration and repositioning on values.

Poverty refers to the absence of attributes, resources, or qualities. Poverty is relative and variously defined in terminology of comparison between cultures, eras, and geographic localities.

In 1900, English researcher, B. Seebohm Rowntree (1951), for the first time recognized the relativity of poverty in his search for an authentic definition of poverty. Rowntree conducted a survey of the population of York to determine the prevalence and causes of poverty. He observed that poverty occurred in families in which the primary wage earner became disabled, departed, or died. Family members were unable to find jobs, often because of an economic depression. Elderly and large families tended to be the poorest. Rowntree identified and distinguished two types of poverty. The primary group contains the poorest individuals and the secondary group contains individuals with adequate incomes who yet lived in poverty. Subsequently, Rowntree developed a concept, the standard of human needs, a level of poverty beneath which a community would intervene to assist its constituents.

The incidence of poverty is high in hierarchical societies where there is a noticeable differentiation between the haves and have nots. The more extreme the differentiation, the greater the incidence of poverty. Governments know that if there is too large an impoverished population, the possibility of revolution increases. As Karl Marx reminded us, the poor and disenfranchised have nothing to lose but their chains. Well-managed bureaucracies work to prevent the revolt by allowing leaders to rise out of poverty and as many poor who can be absorbed by the enemy. Cooption is a continuous process.

Analyst James Hillman (1989) has been most vocal regarding the need to differentiate the true owner of responsibility for situations. The subway train which always runs late is not the fault of the client, the Oedipus complex, or the disfunctioning ego. The fault for the subway train lies within the realm of its regulatory agency. Thus, the proper activity for rectification is not 30 hours of therapy but organizing for social action by writing letters to the agencies and the editors, picketing, and boycotting.

Our consciousness regarding poverty needs to be expanded from our local clientele to all of humankind. The citizens of the world have a choice of quantity of life for the few or for the many. Each territory needs to mine the riches of its mythology to see reflections in the present which can be used as a viable, renewable, salable, natural resource. For instance, an indigenous group in Peru has a centuries-old language with unique characteristics applicable to computers.

Poverty is not erased with a flood of money. The Playboy Foundation has been most articulate to report that the liquidation of their funds to the poor would not redress any inequities. Likewise, major relocation campaigns cause poverty of the spirit and of resources. For instance, there is a program being conducted at this time by the government of Roumania in which whole villages of ancient stone are being bulldozed and families moved to central cities constructed of concrete blocks. Vast histories, linkages, networks, memories, and sensory experiences are leveled. This action, made in the name of poverty and progress, addresses the desire of a government to destroy the historic genius of an indigenous population. There is little recognition here that poverty is addressed through the conscious attending to the whole person, the whole family, the whole community.

Some professionals, most often members of religious orders, address poverty by adopting a life-style of voluntary poverty. These individuals feel that it is immoral for them to live above the poverty level of the folks with whom they work and that diseases born of their malnutrition are badges to be worn with pride. They see their beloved, their God, within the bodies of each person they meet. Two leaders of religious orders in particular dealt with the concept of poverty.

In 1207, St. Francis of Assisi was disowned by his merchant father for repairing a church with his father's resources. He left his parental home "to wed Lady Poverty" and started the Franciscan order with the vows of evangelical freedom, humbleness, and poverty. He and St. Clare, founder of the Poor Ladies, now the Poor Clares, were adamant about their living according to the privilege of poverty. They owned no personal or communal property and lived wholly on alms (Shirley-Price, L., 1959).

Between 1140 and 1150, Hildegard of Bingen (1985) wrote and illustrated her concept of poverty. Poverty is not being without possessions. Rather, poverty is "the spirit of being emptied." In an illumination accompanying the text, Hildegard pictured a path up an iron-colored mountain of salvation, the *axis mundi*, the center of the world on which zeal is expressed through commemoration, mercy, truth, and wholeness. Near the mountain and against a backdrop of a star-studded night-blue sky, stands a human draped in a cream-colored robe which is covered, embodied with eyes. These heterotopic eyes depict the state of consciousness about the unity of life.

I would like to propose a theory. For the past 30 years, professionals in business, development, education, medicine, and social services have applied Abraham Maslow's (1954) hierarchy of needs to work with individuals. I myself taught nurses in the early 1970s how to evaluate the status of a client using Maslow's hierarchy. According to Maslow's theory, individuals must satisfy one level of needs before they can satisfy the next level.

There are five levels of need. The first level includes the basic needs of food, water, and reproductive sex. The second need is shelter. The third need is love and belongingness. The fourth need is self-esteem. The highest need is self-actualization, realization of unity with all life. Maslow believed that individuals satisfied waves of needs. For instance, an individual would be working on obtaining food, water, and reproductive sex primarily and also working on finding shelter. In the past several years, it has been the vogue for individuals to speak of themselves as self-actualized. Actually, Maslow felt that only a few individuals ever achieved self-actualization — such persons as Mahatma Ghandi, Albert Schweitzer, Mother Theresa, and Harriet Tubman.

By the grace of the powers that be, we are blessed to have in our world today populations of aboriginals, humans maintaining as best they can under the assault of technology the life-styles of their original ancestors. Using a highly relative definition of poverty, aboriginals might appear to be poor. Yet, they have been able to live for thousands of years, carefully maintaining a delicate balance between the animal, human, mineral, and plant forms on the lands on which they reside. Aboriginals are able to perpetuate their ecology, in large part, because of their ability to live integrated mental, physical, psychological, and spiritual lives.

Acknowledging Maslow for his very positive contribution to the humanization of our world, I would like to propose an addition to his theory. I propose that we transform the one hierarchical pyramid into two interlocked pyramids, a symbol which mythologists call King Solomon's Seal and the Star of David. As we look at the aboriginal arts and cultures, we see that the survival of the world depends upon the incorporation of the spirit of unity, the concept of self-actualization within every act of life. The acts of obtaining food, water, and reproductive sex, plus shelter need to be interposed with the spirit of thankfulness, celebration, and unity.

We, as professionals, may utilize our heterotopic eyes, consciously choose our values, and act with veracity, climbing the mountain in the center of the world and expressing our zeal for the spirit of unity. A Buddhist story tells that the strongest tree is the tree which bends with the wind. We as professionals need to consider with each gust of the wind our values and our assumptions about poverty. Then we can best address the source of poverty and the integrity of the client.

REFERENCES

Hildegard of Bingen, with Matthew Fox (1985). *Illuminations of Hildegard of Bingen*. Santa Fe, NM: Bear and Company.

Hillman, J. (1989, February). *The feeling of myth*. Public lecture delivered at Columbia University, New York.

Maslow, A. (1970). *Motivation and personality* (2nd ed.). New York, NY: Harper and Row. (Original work published 1954)

Rowntree, B. S., & G. R. Lavers (1951). *Poverty and the welfare state*. New York: Longmans Green.

Sherley-Price, L. (1959). *St. Francis of Assisi: His life and writings as recorded by his contemporaries*. London: A. R. Mowbray.

Inner Poverty:
The Realm of the Hungry Ghost

Anne L. Wissler

SUMMARY. The experience of inner impoverishment is wide-spread in our addictive, externally oriented, rootless cultural collective. The experience is explored with particular reference to themes that emerge when patients are seeking new patterns of living that more accurately feed the urgings of inner longings. Strategies for attuning to and living from the creative unconscious are reflected in efforts by therapist and patient to hear and understand these inner exigencies.

The longings of the soul are never stilled. Incessantly, they beckon us forward. Indeed, life is lived, whether consciously or not, at their mercy. Tracking the course of such longings in psychotherapy includes times for exploring with patients what it takes to make a living: times of musing over what is essential to their usefulness, for vibrant synergy between the energies of inner unfolding and outward manifestation. In some cases, such dialogue springs from struggles to shift a philosophy or way of living from the burnout of one centered in the pursuit of money to a center that engages and harmonizes at more levels of being more of the time. In effect, as one's natural creative resources begin to emerge from shackles of conflict and self-alienation, we must now develop more efficient, psychologically economical, and supportive life patterns that continue to tap and utilize these capacities.

At this edge, we see most clearly the tension between the pull of

Anne L. Wissler, MSW, practices independently in Atlanta, working with individuals, groups, couples, and families. She is Associate Editor of *VOICES: Journal of the American Academy of Psychotherapists.* Mailing address: 315 West Ponce de Leon Avenue, Suite 540, Decatur, GA 30030.

the old, soul-shrouding habits and the building up of strength to shed these for the sake of pioneering choices befitting one's unique journey. The tension is experienced in all spheres from choices of thoughts and actions to priorities for investment of time and energy, in relationships, and in ways of loving and styles of working.

A theme has emerged from working with this tension, which has proven valuable for supporting conscious choice. It derives from descriptions of the soul's journey after separation from the body at death as found in *The Tibetan Book of the Dead* (Fremantle & Trungpa, 1987). Here, as in therapy, the power of naming facilitates conscious choice during the wanderings of the soul in the limbo state. This state mirrors times of living when we are on that unsure ground between death and birth when the old ways no longer suit but the new hasn't yet come. The Book describes six realms or states that the soul traverses, activated by the tendency toward grasping that arises in its confusion. The particular state that coincides with the working up of intense desire is the realm of the hungry ghosts. It is thus described:

> On the fourth day Amitabha and his retinue appear. The bright red light emanating from the heart of Amitabha and his consort is the pure form of the element fire as well as a manifestation of Discriminating Wisdom. It is also the light of skandha which is associated with perception.
>
> . . . At the same time that the brilliant red light shines from Amitabha into your heart center, the dim yellow light of desire and greed streams forth from the realm of hungry ghosts. (Lodö, 1982, pp. 27-29)

In the hungry-ghost realm there is a tremendous feeling of richness, of gathering a lot of possessions; whatever you want you do not have to look for, but you find yourself possessing it. And this makes us more hungry, more deprived, because we get satisfaction not from possessing alone but from searching . . . so there is constant intense hunger which is based not on a sense of poverty but on the realization that we already have everything yet we cannot enjoy it. It is the energy there, the act of exchange, that seems to be more exciting; collecting it, holding it, putting it on, or eating it. That kind of energy is a stimulus, but the grasping quality makes it very awkward. (Trungpa, 1987, pp. 6-7)

[To be] born into the dimension of hungry ghosts [is to] experience unbearable hunger and thirst. No matter how I fulfill myself there, I will never be satisfied. I will be continually hungry and at the same time full. (Gold, 1987, p. 99)

The traveling soul is advised, with the support of meditative readings, to stay with the brilliant clear red light, the purified element of fire, the discriminating wisdom light. This is done through conscious, finely honed concentration, by sustaining a sense of longing in an attitude of faith and non-action. The concurrent appearance of the alluring soft-yellow-light path attracts unconscious habituated tendencies that have accumulated through dominant experiences of intense desire. It inspires fear of the brilliantly clear, discriminating red ray and beckons toward the dulling, blissful pleasure of indiscriminant, habitual action. It sweeps the unenlightened voyager into the repetitive cycling that is the hungry-ghost realm.

CLINICAL PHENOMENOLOGY

The experience of intense desiring, of wishes to consume or devour, and of grasping and possessiveness are ubiquitous in psychotherapy as impulses long suppressed resurface in the patient's living and awareness. Much sensitivity and discernment may be required by therapist and patient in working this territory, however. Since the norm in our cultural collective is so oriented to owning and possessing, it may be difficult to perceive the growth-defeating aspects of such patterns. In many ways we are trained to meet life's vicissitudes by consuming, by taking in or putting on from outside ourselves that which will reputedly and quickly feed our hunger, comfort our anxiety, numb our pain, alter our mood. Based on such observations, some have justifiably described our culture as an addictive one (Beattie, 1987; Schaef, 1986; Woodman, 1982, 1987, 1989), viewing the majority of individuals and institutions as "codependent" upon each other's growth-stunting habituated behavior. And in the dispirited morass that addictive behavior begets, the integrity of the organically unfolding journey of the embodied soul is lost. The resulting hunger that sets in, when one knows not what one wants, nor what is meaningful in life, is of the spirit, a spiritual impoverishment.

Words, images, and actions brought forth by patients that suggest this condition indicate an aroused concern about the self which is not necessarily self-consciously spiritual at all. In the course of extricating himself from relational stresses that brought him into therapy, Kevin had developed more esteem for his reclaimed beleaguered self. His determination to "do it differently" fueled the pursuit of self-reflective awareness. In this session, he noted signs of overload closing in on him, "too many irons in the fire." This is a spot he cycled through periodically. In desperation, he would declare a moratorium on any involvement until the discomfort eased through task completion. He wondered if perhaps he just couldn't say "No."

As I heard his experience this time, my persistent sense of him was that ages had passed since anyone, including Kevin himself, had asked him, "What do *you* like to do?" or "How would you *like* to spend this time?" or "How's this *experience* for you?" In response to my sharing this, he gave several examples of how much the range of his experience was mediated by the look in the other's eyes, and then narrowed by his interpretation of that. This kept him from the direct impact of information generated through his own eyes and other senses. In this light, his "many irons in the fire" offered hit-or-miss attempts to broaden the range of satisfying experiences by drawing more possibilities to himself. But while providing himself many chances to discover felt meaning, much was lost to this external mediation process. By detouring his connection with himself, he missed the fullness of the experience, the information thus generated, and the chance to savor his own feedback. His consuming-without-savoring left him perpetually hungry. Because he was not thriving on his own experiences, he exuded a ghostly sort of absence from an apparently lived life.

Judy had been distant from her mother since she was a teenager. She was now, at forty-three, working on an adult-to-adult rapprochement as part of her own inner healing. In a session that occurred while her mother was visiting, Judy spoke of feeling herself recoil when her mother delightedly exclaimed, "Oh, this will be OUR day!" It was a time free of activities or friends Judy had invited to divide up their earlier days. Moving more into that feeling now, Judy faced all the intensity of her hungry mother bearing down on her to do something, fearing there was nothing, even to extreme self-sacrifice, she could do to fill that awful grasping yearning. Typically, such feelings activated old defensive patterns based in the belief that preserving herself required fighting her mother off. This time, she had a dream. The image was the face of an elderly figure with strikingly androgynous features—thick gray hair curling gently around the ears, plaintively wise yet frightened eyes sunk deep within their sockets, stooped shoulders, shuffling gait, and layers of years-worn clothing. As escort, Judy was to take this person around the city to places they might enjoy. Yet wherever they went, her companion was preoccupied with feeling cold and could not participate. Finally, Judy found a restaurant and fed her friend tea and hot soup which evoked a warmed and brighter response.

As Judy explored the dream, she was stunned to recognize the androgynous figure as a part of herself that her mother, due to Judy's childhood experience of her, had long carried and now mirrored back to Judy. In a subsequent session, Judy felt herself straining toward me with the same hungry intensity she'd felt from her mother, as if I had something that she knew she needed to go within to find. She noted how she had been arranging her life based on things she thought would be enjoyable, ignoring physical and emotional signals that suggested the plans she had based in logic were not tending her deeper need. Her hunger was a soul-level hunger that would require entering into deeper dialogue with it through such resources as body sensations, dreams, imagination, ritual, and other creative processes.

Carla dreamed she was at an old stone labyrinthine structure which looked like ancient ruins shimmering in the moonlight. She was stalking around its outer walls looking for an opening through which to enter and find a vulnerable party whom she could engage as a lover. Anne (her therapist) was following her around at a distance far enough to allow her to explore and experiment but vigilant to make sure she didn't get in or get attached anywhere. The dream came at a time in Carla's work when she had opened herself deeply to the unequivocal intensity of her hunger to be mothered in literal, physical, and primitive ways: to be held, fed, stroked, carried, protected, rocked, comforted. These feelings had been lost to her awareness by dissociative, intense, yet brief sexual encounters with figures construed in her fantasy as maternal. While her feelings were quelled or numbed through such actions, the backlash of recriminations and loss of self afterwards left her feeling more impoverished than before. In contrast, the claiming of feelings in the dream resulted in an unexpected sense of fullness in self-reconciliation. Paradoxically, tapping into the intense longing she'd thought would feel unbearably depriving brought the fulfillment of self-contact she had missed. Her internalization of Anne as dream symbol represented her now present guardian of this new and tenuous response. What she said was empowering: "When I'm out in space untethered to myself, not internal, whatever I do is not enough, I can't get satisfied; when I'm with myself, my work is enough, my connections with people are enough, I'm not consumed with desperate, voracious desires for sex or obsessed with worries about money."

In each of these instances the hungry-ghost motif has been active. There is accumulating without consuming, consuming that is not nourishing, searching cut short by grasping, and holding on that creates a sense of fullness while depotentiating the search which might in itself energize and satisfy.

BEYOND WEALTH: RETRIEVING BEN'S HUNGRY GHOST

Ben came into therapy at forty, furious with all whom he cast as authorities over himself—his wife, his father, certain friends, and before long, me. There was certainly a functional side to his projection. His early life's relational climate had been so confused and chaotic that he needed an external authority with enough grounding and inner esteem to help him contain and consolidate his internalized fragmentation. By then, he'd accumulated much pain from grabbing on too heartily to what he once called "rosebushes"—dazzling persons who attracted him and turned prickly, insecure, rigid, and exploitative when he got close, replicating his experience with parents of childhood.

Ben's father was a frustrated artist who made it big in manufacturing by the time Ben was ten. Left by Ben's mother long before, he then blossomed into the aloof, controlling, glad-handing, distrustful playboy he remained by insulating himself from others with wealth and a coterie of yes-men that eventually included Ben. The emotional support for Ben's role, which amounted to a high-class corporate valet, came from Ben's puer projection of his inner hero which father was happy to embrace, as well as Ben's penchant for drama and role play. This defensive package was balanced out by his enactment of what he called his own identity, designed in strict countercultural opposition to all that he imagined his father approved. Neither role reflected or expressed the unadulterated essence of Ben himself. He seemed forever the adolescent, crippled by his addiction to father's wealth.

Then, after years of emotionally isolated overdrive, his father succumbed to chronic physical ailments and died. He left Ben the full-time job of sorting and settling his tangled affairs and large assets. Ben had never sought out his own means of support. But now he faced the psychological task of carving out an existence based not on the need to earn a living, but in some inner urge — could we resurrect it? — to move toward living from the exigencies of his own essence.

For a time, Ben stayed close to his hero-father by living out his father's life — though he never would have called it that — of flashy fun and reckless escapism, travel, women, cars, booze, and various pseudo-macho ways of calling attention to himself. His therapy was consumed with self-absorbed tales of his chaotic childhood, buttressed with sophisticated defenses from his psychology classes and weekend encounter groups. It was during a couple's session of that era that his long-winded psycho-legalese response to my feelingful question finally provoked me beyond customary propriety. I yelled at him with an intensity that shocked us both, something to the effect of asking him to cut the crap and get real. There was a long silence. We carried on in some fashion, though I wondered afterward if he would come in and terminate next session. In fact, he told me he'd not read of anyone doing that in any of his psychotherapy books, not even Carl Whitaker who wrestled the adolescent son in family therapy. He wondered, maybe his wife could learn to do that, too?

The tide had turned. If I could be real, perhaps he could, too. Slowly, he began to trade in his rules, judgments, counterdependent defenses, and hostile actings-out for a gentler, more compassionate recognition of his vulnerability. Though his bank account could support his fragmented lifestyle, his anxiety and hunger for connection with others and with himself could not. Though his marriage foundered, he couldn't give it up. And the safer he got in therapy the more he intimated, then heard clearly, his lack of direction and the shame and grief he felt in that. Like the prodigal returned, he at last confronted his true malaise: He had yet to fully embrace his own quest, to experience his own heroism.

Though much of what he needed to retrieve came from the thawing of frozen memories, the birth of his dream life was significant. His dreams bridged his awareness from the externalization to which he was so prone back to subtle aspects of his internal world he couldn't have claimed if not generated in his own material. As he struggled to introduce and sustain creative activity, he dreamed often of poor black people—babies, orphans, men, women—he had to protect, support, and defend. There was longing in his voice as he described his longtime friendship with a poor black family whose matriarch he admired for her bonding with the earth "where she gets strength and solidness that enables her to withstand hardships of poverty." I thought of Jung's (1961) comment on the rootlessness pervading American culture; here, alienation from unconscious primitivity is the danger for every person who has lost touch with the dark maternal earthy ground of his or her being. Ben's financial aid of this family mirrored the support he was lending his inner creative unconscious. This had heretofore been carried externally by important women and was little known within. The intimacy and modeling he gained from these people tapped a grounded, wise sense of himself and his basic needs that the internalization of his father's preoccupation with the material world had eclipsed.

Indeed, it was at this point of rekindling his own creative fire that the pull to distract himself into old places became most severe. He explored this in a cycle of three dreams, which occurred after he canceled an appointment when his wife wanted him to do something else:

1. I was in an office building which reminded me of my father's building, but I was my present age.
   There was an outside stairway like a fire escape by my office. Underneath my office is a person I can see inside his window looking up at me who is attractive to me because he looks quite heroic. But I detest his bigotry: He says awful things to black passers-by.
   I go outside to meet Sue (wife) for lunch. A black person goes by and the man shouts obscenities. I get furious and confront him. He puts on his coat and says "I'll see about that . . ." I'm terrified what will happen.
   An Eastern stewardess goes by on her way to the airport. I want to go too. I'm afraid Sue will see me.
   The stewardess tells me there's a van that picks up anyone at any place every 15 minutes. And I think toward her employer, "No wonder you're going broke. You can't do that."

2. I was with Sue and the kids in the car going to my therapy appointment. We stopped at an English village west of the city so they could do some shopping.
   It came time for my appointment and they weren't ready so I left. Heading east, I saw the city skyline, but when I got downtown there were no exits, which surprised me.
   Looking south (opposite direction from therapist's office) I saw the ocean. I was surprised and thought, "This must be a dream." But I was excited to find such a quick way to the ocean. When I got there it was muddy and there were thick clouds offshore obscuring the view.

3. A man gives me a golf ball he says I can drive 336 yards, and it works. But 336 is a bad number, something to do with witchcraft.
   The scene changes and it is night. In the darkness I see a large,

almost silhouetted figure of a primitive-looking man holding a lit candle. Behind him is a huge blazing red and yellow fire. He looks like Lucifer but his face is plaintive and pleading. He looks gentle, lost and agonizing in this place.

These dreams were tough to bring forth, hard for him to remember and then hard to recall when in session. They presaged an inner shift. On first reporting the second dream, Ben was totally enamored of being at the ocean, where his mother took him in childhood. But it wasn't hard for him to see how this fantasy spot was a place of obscured vision, luring him away from where he intended and wanted to be when he succumbed to it. As in the first dream, when he indulged his escapist wish to fly away with the ungrounded feminine, he was distracted from the guardianship of his own earthy wisdom from the false outer hero. Such a path could leave him creatively bankrupt. The third dream offered an image from the realm of the soul (feminine/witchcraft) that will take him far (long-driving golf ball conferred upon him by the man). The setting is natural, the figure humble. Like a man on a vision quest for initiation into his mature self, he is keeping vigil by the fire, piercing the dark places with his own light, facing the plaintive, pleading, deeply resounding inner longings. He felt compassion for the figure whom he spoke of as his soulmate "crying out from the depths." The depth of feeling reflected his own truth in a way that clearly exposed the earlier distractions.

The immediate impact on his living was to notice how his unguarded time left him wide open to distractions. This dashed the just-budding tender inner connections that could support his pursuit of personal creative power. Knowing this, he could choose to manage himself in ways that protected inner unfolding. His terror, once to be avoided, became a challenge for stretching himself more into life, for example, by standing up for what he knew from within. He fondly recalled that just as the fire of anger once burned off the obscuring transference earlier in our relationship, so now the welling-up of his passion could guide him to choices reflecting his own discriminating wisdom.

STRATEGIES AND IMPLICATIONS

Work with Ben and others reveals that a key aspect in shifting the hungry ghost dynamic from endless cycles of desiring, acquiring, consuming, and burning is the capacity to discriminate experiences of life-supporting longing from signals of acute deprivation or unmet need. The ache that stretches our capacity for creative emptiness is qualitatively distinct from the stinging pain of wounding. Irritations of breaking new ground are to be distinguished from the irritation-rage of the thwarted search which may suggest we are recycling in the hungry-ghost realm. These discriminations are honed, as *The Tibetan Book of the Dead* suggests, when we tolerate the refining fire, when we forego the familiar yet ultimately frustrating grasping/consuming tactics and hold out for the hope of that which fulfills more deeply and truly. Inner impoverishment of spirit is nourished by reaching toward that which feeds spirit, not by accumulations of matter.

We move toward nourishment of spirit by understanding and steering clear of demands of hungry ghosts past, burning off what is no longer relevant, layer by layer, so as to retrieve and cultivate a connection with the inner voice of our deepest longing. As the grounded ego learns to provide a sturdy container of body-mind working in unity, the task becomes one of surrender to that voice. This longing is the experience that ecstatic poets Rumi (13th cen.) and Kabir (15th cen.) describe as akin to passionate love, the soaring soul embodied in a self-aware state of surrender: keeping company with the Guest within. Such longing becomes the centerpiece, the orienting ally, from which life's richest course is lived.

In the context of our American cultural collective where the wisdom of non-action, the stillness of introspection, and the subtle process of slowly crafted results tend not to be honored, valuing the efforts of staying with our longings until they teach us what to do is a huge challenge. Psychotherapy creates a powerful holding environment for this revolutionary inner shift by providing patient support, active mirroring feedback that bridges toward the patient's own new ways, unswerving trust of inner process, and love of the mysteries of the soul in its splendid voyage. As the patient internalizes the capacity to hold to, value, and recognize the signals of his or her own process, life becomes more of a creative adventure; there is a sense of being lived in harmony with self and with the larger forces of the universe. In the fullness of tracking one's true quest lies the opportunity to relive spiritual, and thus material, poverty from inner and outer worlds.

REFERENCES

Beattie, M. (1987). *Codependent no more*. Center City, MN: Hazeldon.

Fremantle, F., & Trungpa, C. (Trans.). (1987). *The Tibetan book of the dead*. Boston: Shambhala.

Gold, E.J. (1987). *American book of the dead*. Nevada City, CA: IDHHB, Inc.

Goodrich-Dunn, B. (1989). The conscious feminine — an interview with Marion Woodman. *Common Boundary*, 7(2), 10-17.

Jung, C.G. (1961). *Memories, dreams, reflections*. New York: Pantheon.

Lodö, V.L. (1982). *Bardo teachings: The way of death and rebirth*. Ithaca, NY: Snow Lion Publications.

Schaef, A.W. (1986). *Co-dependence: Misunderstood-mistreated*. San Francisco: Harper and Row.

Woodman, M. (1982). *Addiction to perfection*. Toronto: Inner City Books.

Woodman, M. (1987). Worshipping illusions. *Parabola*, *12*(2), 56-67.

Counseling the Impoverished Rural Client: Issues for Family Therapists

Thomas V. Sayger
Kevin O. Heid

SUMMARY. This article discusses the issues facing impoverished families in rural communities and the therapists providing services for them. Information is provided regarding roadblocks to successful treatment, strengths of impoverished rural families, and suggestions for treatment programs.

When one thinks of this nation's poor, images of the urban homeless, families trapped in inner-city slums, transients, or migrant workers often come to mind. Although these images are certainly valid and necessitate the attention of our society and profession, it is the purpose of this article to focus on the plight of the rural poor. The rural poor, like the urban poor, are a heterogeneous group. Poverty has been a persistent problem in rural areas for many years. In the late 1950s, approximately one-third of all non-urban resi-

---

Thomas V. Sayger, PhD, is Assistant Professor of Counseling Psychology and Counselor Education at the University of Wisconsin-Madison and a Licensed Psychologist. He has published in the area of family psychology. Mailing address: Department of Counseling Psychology and Counselor Education, University of Wisconsin-Madison, 349D Education Building, 1000 Bascom Mall, Madison, WI 53706.

Kevin O. Heid, MEd, is a doctoral candidate in counseling psychology at Washington State University and Psychology Intern at Spokane Community Mental Health Center, Spokane, WA. Mailing address: Department of Counseling Psychology, Washington State University, Pullman, WA 99164-2131.

Appreciation is extended to the John F. Kennedy Library, Boston, MA, for their assistance in obtaining resource materials.

161

dents lived in poverty and comprised over 50 percent of all the American poor (United States Advisory Commission on Rural Poverty, 1968). Subsequently, as a result of national economic improvement and expanded social welfare programs, the rate of rural poverty decreased between 1959 and 1979. Today, however, poverty continues to be a severe problem in rural areas despite the public perception of poverty as an urban concern (Deaver, Hoppe, & Ross, 1986). Additionally, with the increasing plight of the American farmer, the numbers of rural poor continue to remain significant.

The problems of the poor are some of the more complex issues facing American society today. Annually, both the public and private sectors expend vast amounts of money and time attempting to serve the needs of this country's economically disadvantaged population. Public welfare agencies and many private charitable organizations strive to efficaciously attend to the basic needs of the nation's poor, while sociological and psychological research continues to focus upon the etiological and epidemiological bases of poverty. Yet, poverty continues despite the efforts of organizations, agencies, and individuals.

Millions of people throughout this country will not be wondering where they will spend their annual vacation or purchase a car. They do not concern themselves with issues regarding middle-management promotions, savings for retirement, or designer apparel. Millions of impoverished Americans will today wonder how they will feed themselves and their children.

Although improvements in the treatment of and attention to the needs of the nation's poor have occurred, more can be done. Kennedy (1963, April), in a letter to the United State Senate, stated:

> Poverty in the midst of plenty is a paradox that must not go unchallenged in this country. Ours is the wealthiest of nations, yet one-sixth of our people live below minimal levels of health, housing, food, and education—in the slums of cities, in migratory labor camps, in economically depressed areas, on Indian reservations. In addition, special hardships are faced by our senior citizens, dependent children, and the victims of

mental illness, mental retardation, and other disabling misfortunes. (pp. 320-321)

The United States government defines poverty as existing when there is too little cash income to cover minimum levels of consumption (Ghelfi & Saupe, 1986). Although thresholds seem to vary by demographic characteristics (e.g., family size, age, culture), lack of income is the common variable which disallows poverty-stricken families to meet basic physiological and survival needs. Poverty is a national tragedy that impacts all of American society. As mental health professionals are called upon to respond to the psychological needs of the nation's poor, counselors, psychologists, social workers, and psychiatrists must educate themselves about the plight of the impoverished client. It appears that those families and individuals who are least able to avail themselves of psychological services are the same people who are in the greatest need of such programs. Poverty can be a victimizing phenonomenon and, while being careful not to blame the victim, psychological professionals must recognize the complete implications of this form of victimization on many of our elderly, children, and families.

Rodgers and Weiher (1986) suggest that the rural poor can be contrasted with the urban poor on several dimensions. Typically, the rural poor are more likely than the urban poor to live in a two-parent household, to be elderly, to be the "working poor," and to suffer from hunger, malnutrition, health problems, and learning difficulties. The rural poor also tend to be Caucasian, poorly educated, and less likely to receive social services. As a result of the social isolation that exists in many rural communities, impoverished rural clients are less likely to band together to form advocacy coalitions for the purpose of enlightenment of the public and protection of their peer group.

Sundet and Mermelstein (1987), in a study of impoverished rural families, identified their most critical needs. These researchers identified counseling services as the most critical need for nearly 20 percent of the rural impoverished families surveyed and over 7 percent of these families were identified as being too clinically depressed to seek services. The impoverished disorganized family tends to mesh into an undifferentiated whole (Minuchin & Montalvo, 1967), thus creating an "us vs. them" attitude which harbors feelings of denial, mistrust, and dependency. Therapy, in this instance, should focus on individuation of family members and family subgroups to encourage and expand emotional involvement in the treatment process. Other barriers to obtaining counseling services, as cited by Sundet and Mermelstein (1987), were lack of awareness of service availability, embarrassment, and skepticism regarding the quality of services.

Many impoverished rural families may, in fact, have more limited access to services and programs than the urban poor. Transportation to the nearest service provider may be problematic and many rural poor families never receive mental health services because of geographical constriction. Mental health professionals may want to consider the merit of home-based/outreach counseling services for some clients.

In addition to difficulties created by isolation and lack of transportation, many rural poor families "fall through the cracks" of available human service systems and remain untreated. This may result from the fact that impoverished families cannot afford to pay an hourly fee for services or do not meet the criteria for client acceptance at local community mental health centers. In essence, many of those who might avail themselves of mental health care either find themselves too poor to afford it, or are not sufficiently disturbed to qualify for services.

A myriad of reasons may operate to discourage the entry of many rural impoverished families into the counseling relationship. Few would argue that persistent poverty or the continuous lack of resources and control over one's life would negatively affect one's attitude toward one's world and one's place in it. A "learned helplessness" attitude may suggest that persistently poor individuals tend not to seek counseling services because they perceive having no solutions or hope for overcoming their financial distress. The family therapist may want to make an initial assessment of the client's readiness for change (Horne & Sayger, in press) to determine which resources the client has available.

Gurin and Gurin (1970) characterized the importance of expectancy theory as it relates to the condition of the poor. This theory suggests that motivation consists of two parts: (1) the desirability of an outcome; and (2) the expectancy that one's own action can assist in the attainment of the outcome of choice. If a chronically unemployed individual perceives that job search will have little or no positive outcome, he or she may very well discontinue employment seeking behaviors. The action may not be an issue of desire to work, but becomes a matter of expectation as the individual anticipates an inability to exercise control over his or her life situation.

Similarly, many impoverished rural families may avoid seeking necessary mental health services not because of a lack of motivation, but because of a lack of expectation that the intervention will produce any positive outcome. In these cases, such refusal is not predicated on lack of desire for assistance, but rather on doubt regarding possibility for change.

Kane (1987) reported positive correlations between earnings and family income and positive beliefs in personal efficacy, personal control, and future orientation. Fear of failure was negatively correlated with earnings and family income. It is suggested that such personal beliefs in efficacy and control are in part a result of past and current control over resources.

Empowerment of the client is an important aspect of therapy with the rural poor. Clients need to be involved in the development of realistic and achievable treatment plans. This participation will serve as an opportunity for the client to actually experience control over the change process. Clients should have a voice in determining the length of sessions, frequency of contact, duration of treatment program, and establishment of goals.

Fleischman, Horne, and Arthur (1983) suggest that family therapists for low-income families may actually find themselves assuming the role of caseworker, as well as therapist, and devoting time or special sessions to providing information on available services. Fleischer (1977) asserts that traditional intervention techniques may be ineffective with impoverished families and that therapy must often be supplemented by the mobilization of community resources. The family therapist can be an excellent resource for information regarding such community services as public assistance programs, clothing banks, food banks, food-stamp programs, legal aid, and many others.

Mental health professionals are encouraged to attend to the

health/physiological, economic, psychosocial, intellectual, and financial needs of impoverished clients. Without this holistic and multidisciplinary approach, treatment professionals run the risk of missing the most pressing needs of the client. Professionals cannot assume that they know what is "in the best interest of the client" for to do so one may inadvertently victimize the very client that one is attempting to empower.

The following lists are offered as aids to the family therapist working with impoverished rural families. These lists are not intended to be all-encompassing, but simply suggestions for assessing and treating this underserved population.

Roadblocks to Successful Treatment

1. Social stigma associated with seeking psychological support.
2. Financial inflexibilities: transportation costs, childcare expenses, etc.
3. Lack of social support, isolation, insularity.
4. Lack of community resources.
5. Sense of "us vs. them": family co-dependency.
6. Lack of future or success orientation; sense of being trapped and unable to rise above poverty.
7. Social stigma of being poor.
8. Lack of individuation of family members; unclear boundaries; enmeshment.

Strengths of Impoverished Rural Families

1. Survivor attitude: live from day to day, will do the best they can with what they've got.
2. Typically have ready access to extended family network and friends.
3. Creativity: have learned to survive with minimal resources.
4. Can raise partial food supply; working the land.
5. Family members form their own social support system within the family.

Suggestions for Treatment Programs

1. Utilize home-based/outreach programs.
2. Provide pro bono services or use sliding-fee scale based upon income.
3. Establish expectations for success.
4. Empower the client.
5. Develop achievable and realistic goals.
6. Achieve normal individuation of family members and subgroups.
7. Determine level of client readiness for change: employment status, social support system, legal status, agency involvement, commitment to treatment, etc.
8. Access fathers and extended family members for support.
9. Assist clients in finding resources to fulfill minimal health/safety needs: welfare, food banks, clothing banks, food stamps, etc.
10. Align with physicians to address concerns of social stigma to seeking psychological services (clients typically present with physical concerns because it is more socially and personally acceptable); utilize office space in medical facilities.
11. Be aware of professional biases against the poor: "Poor people aren't intelligent," "poor people can achieve much," etc.
12. Give the client the benefit of the doubt: Is it resistance or a genuine inability to succeed at the assigned task?
13. Provide a multidisciplinary treatment approach; access other social service agencies and community support systems.

Accessing and effectively treating the impoverished rural family is a challenge that faces many mental health professionals. The problems are complex; however, the barriers are not insurmountable. In order to more effectively address the mental health needs of impoverished rural clients, more mental health professionals must commit themselves to the task of assisting these families. These clients may need to be invited to actively participate in the system, require holistic and multidisciplinary treatment programs, and must be involved in the development of their treatment plan. As is true of all clients, the rural poor expect, and deserve, to be treated with dignity, sensitivity, compassion, and heightened professionalism.

REFERENCES

Deaver, K. L., Hoppe, R. A., & Ross, P. J. (1986). Public policy and rural poverty: A view from the 1980's. *Policy Studies Journal, 15*, 291-309.

Fleischer, G. (1977). Techniques for working with disorganized low socioeconomic families. *American Journal of Orthopsychiatry, 37*, 880-887.

Fleischman, M. J., Horne, A. M., & Arthur, J. (1983). *Troubled families: A treatment program*. Champaign, IL: Research Press.

Ghelfi, L. M., & Saupe, W. E. (1986). Policy implications of the economics of farm family poverty in the United States. *Policy Studies Journal, 15*, 311-325.

Gurin, G., & Gurin, P. (1970). Expectancy theory in the study of poverty. *Journal of Social Issues, 26*, 83-104.

Horne, A. M., & Sayger, T. V. (in press). *Treating conduct and oppositional defiant disorders in children*. New York: Pergamon Press.

Kane, T. J. (1987). Giving back control: Long-term poverty and motivation. *Social Service Review, 61*,. 407-419.

Kennedy, J. F. (1963, April). *In the midst of plenty* (Public papers of the President, John F. Kennedy, Item 130, 320-321). Boston: John F. Kennedy Library.

Minuchin, S., & Montalvo, B. (1967). Techniques for working with disorganized low socioeconomic families. *American Journal of Orthopsychiatry, 37*, 880-887.

Rodgers, H. J., Jr., & Weiher, G. (1986). The rural poor in America: A statistical overview. *Policy Studies Journal, 15*, 279-289.

Sundet, P. A., & Mermelstein, J. (1987). Why aren't farmers banging down agency doors? *Public Welfare, 45*, 15-19.

United States Advisory Commission on Rural Poverty. (1968). *Rural poverty in the United States: A report*. Washington: United State Government Printing Office.

Clinical Applications of a Control Model of Psychological Health: Two Case Studies of Stress-Related Disorders

Deane H. Shapiro, Jr.

SUMMARY. The applications of one aspect of a control model of psychological health are illustrated by the use of two cases referred for stress-related disorders. This model involves four quadrants describing dimensions of control: quadrant one (active control, positive assertive); quadrant two (letting go control, positive yielding); quadrant three (overcontrol, negative assertive); and quadrant four (too little control, negative yielding). Increased psychological health is presumed to occur when scores for quadrants one and two increase; and scores for quadrants three and four decrease. These two cases, though presenting quite different pre-test profiles, revealed rather consistent post-test changes in the expected direction. Follow-up data showed varying degrees of relapse. The discussion section suggests additional areas which future research needs to examine in order to develop a more comprehensive control based model of psychotherapy.

God grant me the serenity
to accept the things I cannot change,
the courage to change the things I can,
and the wisdom to know the difference.

— Reinhold Niebuhr

Deane H. Shapiro, Jr., PhD, is a Diplomate, American Board of Professional Psychology (Clinical Specialty), and Associate Professor in Residence in the Department of Psychiatry and Human Behavior, California College of Medicine, University of California-Irvine, Irvine, CA 92717.

Hans Selye (1974), in a now classic formulation, suggested that there was both good stress (eu-stress, for euphoric); and bad stress (distress). Research has shown that chronic, unrelenting stress is associated with a variety of mental and physical disorders (Elliot, 1984; Friedman & Ulmer, 1984; Jacob & Chesney, 1984; Pelletier, 1977). A central question becomes, therefore, what distinguishes positive stress from negative stress.

A convincing amount of data is accumulating which suggests that a major answer to that question is "a sense of control" (Rodin, 1986) over the stress (Shapiro, Evans, & Shapiro, 1987). Simultaneous with this research on perceived control, clinicians and scientists were attempting to develop and refine a variety of non-pharmacological strategies which could be used to give clients and patients more control over their own attitudes and behaviors. Collectively, these techniques (which include, but are not limited to, self-hypnosis, biofeedback, behavioral self-control, meditation, autogenic training, guided imagery), may be subsumed under the label self-control strategies (Shapiro & Shapiro, 1980; Shapiro & Zifferblatt, 1976).

Current research on self-control strategies, however, appears to have reached a plateau. Although it is clear, based on clinical and physiological measures, that certain self-control strategies are more effective than a placebo control group, research (with few exceptions) has not yet been able to differentiate between competing self-control strategies as a treatment of choice for a particular clinical problem (Shapiro, 1982). Further, for certain clinical disorders (such as alcoholism, smoking, obesity) self-control strategies alone appear, as yet, to be relatively ineffective long term; and, in addition, the adherence/compliance rate with these strategies is quite low (Brownell, Marlatt, Lichtenstein, & Wilson, 1986; Jeffery, 1987; Nathan, 1986).

Given this situation, what are clinicians and psychotherapists to do when dealing with individuals suffering from conditions relating to impairments in the realm of human control?

There are several different avenues being explored in this author's work in order to deal with this dilemma. As a guiding principle, current efforts are attempting to develop, and then integrate, a broad-based theory of human control with a clinically relevant control-based model of psychotherapy. This approach should eventually help us refine and make more precise the matching of the use of particular self-control strategies to a given patient with a given clinical problem.

At the most theoretical level, this effort involves refining the construct of control into component dimensions: choice, awareness, discipline, goal, responsibility, and skill (Shapiro, 1983a; Shapiro & Shapiro, 1979); to explore relevant aspects (species) of a control theory: including fears of loss of control; the concept of a need for control; belief in ability to gain control (Shapiro & Bates, 1989); the cultural and sex-role bias inherent in the term self-control, and its relationship to psychological health and social desirability (Shapiro, 1985); and the role of "cultural" assumptions in our understanding and development of (self)-control (Shapiro, 1989a). At the other end of the continuum, the work involves a systems approach to the clinical context in which the use of self-control strategies occurred. Dimensions of this systems model include therapist variables (i.e., orientation, views of self-control, knowledge of the strategies, etc.); client variables (i.e., motivation, responsibility, etc.); relationship variables; assessment of clinical concern; selection of the self-control strategy; teaching of the strategy; adherence and compliance, and follow up (Shapiro, 1983b).

In an ideal world, these two ends of the continuum would meet somewhere in the middle, and work in perfect complementarity. Unfortunately, the research literature in psychology (often involving single variable interventions) frequently isn't sufficiently rich to provide complete-enough information to deal with an actual clinical case; and the clinical cases are often too complex and idiosyncratic to allow generalization clinically or satisfactory inductive theory building.

What is presented in this article is an effort to bridge those two ends of the continuum along one aspect of a control model of psychological health. In particular, this article focuses on how a four quadrant model of control can be used as an assessment device to measure patient's self-perceived "control" identity and issues, and as a way to help determine therapeutic change as a result of self-control interventions.

Both cases described were referred for stress-related disorders.

However, as is evident from the cases, the causes of the stress problems were quite different. This required a refining of the goal of therapy for each person, and consequently a relatively different emphasis on the type of self-control strategies used.

METHODOLOGY

Subjects and Setting

Subjects were individuals who were seen in Northern California while the author worked in the Bay Area near San Francisco. Each case is reported separately (giving relevant demographic and clinical information). Pre and post tests utilizing the four quadrant control instrument were given at the beginning and at the end of individual therapy, as well as at a follow-up.

The Four-Quadrant Control Instrument (Mode)

In the introduction to this article, it was noted that the variable which may be most responsible for distinguishing positive from negative stress is the sense of control. Based on a theoretical framework evolving from work in Eastern and Western psychologies (Shapiro, 1978; 1983c), it was argued that there were really two ways in which individuals could develop a positive sense of control. One way was an assertive, active mode of control in which the person tried, in a goal-oriented, instrumental way to alter or change the situation (referred to as quadrant one). And a second way was a yielding, accepting, letting-go mode of control in which the person tried to accept things as they were, without changing them (referred to as quadrant two).[1] Quadrant one was thought to be most effective when the situation was potentially under the person's active control ("the courage to change the things I can"); and quadrant two was thought to be the most effective strategy when the situation was not under the person's control ("accept the things I cannot change").

Two additional quadrants were also posited. Quadrant three was identified as the negative aspect of assertiveness (overcontrol, aggressiveness); and quadrant four defined as the negative aspect of quadrant two (timidity, too little control). (See Table One.)

TABLE ONE. A Four-Quadrant Model of Control

QUADRANT ONE	QUADRANT TWO
ACTIVE CONTROL POSITIVE ASSERTIVE	LETTING-GO CONTROL POSITIVE YIELDING ACCEPTING
QUADRANT THREE	**QUADRANT FOUR**
OVER-CONTROL NEGATIVE ASSERTIVE	TOO LITTLE CONTROL NEGATIVE YIELDING

Words were generated reflecting each of the four quadrants, and then rater reliability was obtained by having six experts rate the words along four dimensions. The raters were male and female experts in three fields germane to the instrument: East/West psychology; sex role psychology; and Type A behavior. Only words which received an 83.33% (5 out of 6) agreement were kept in the final instrument (Shapiro, 1982a).

This instrument was then given to over 2000 individuals in 11 cities across the United States to develop a normative profile for high (and low) psychological health[2] (Shapiro, 1983e); for self-control (Shapiro, 1983d); and to compare those profiles with a social-desirability profile (Shapiro, 1985). (See Figure One.)

In the current study subjects were asked to rate themselves on the instrument using a four point Likert scale (from "describes me not well at all," to "describes me extremely well"). After they completed the self-description, subjects were instructed to go back and evaluate each answer, saying whether they would like to stay the same, be more that way, or less that way. In so doing, they provided information similar to a real/ideal questionnaire, as well as a "self-satisfaction," or "self-acceptance" quotient. Quadrant averages reflect a total score per quadrant divided by the number of words in the quadrant. The "overall satisfaction" score is the number of "stay the same" answers across all four quadrants.

FIGURE ONE. Normative Profile of Psychological Health

Shapiro Self-Control
Inventory (SSCI)

In addition to the four-quadrant control instrument, subjects also completed the SSCI.[3] This inventory, which is in its third revision, is still in the exploratory stages of development. It consists of two parts. Part one involves contextual information, including demographic and personal background, as well as four subscales (beliefs and expectations about personal self-control and ability to change; motivation; resistance; and responsibility). The second part looks at four specific areas: intimacy, yielding and acceptance, overcontrol, and personal style.

This inventory is primarily helpful from a heuristic, descriptive standpoint at this stage of its development. Some of the questions are in Likert format; some are open ended to gather more complete information as part of a structured therapeutic interview.

Techniques and Therapeutic Style

The author's views about the process of therapy and the context within which self-control techniques should be used are not discussed here as they have been detailed elsewhere (Shapiro, 1980, chapter 4; Shapiro, 1983b). In both cases, after the initial self-observation and data gathering phase, some combination of cognitive behavioral and/or meditative techniques were used initially. These techniques have also been described in detail elsewhere (Shapiro 1977; 1978; 1978a; 1980; Shapiro & Zifferblatt, 1976). Additional techniques utilized as part of the therapeutic intervention for a given patient are described in the actual case write-up.

CASE PRESENTATIONS AND RESULTS

Case One: Art P.

The client, Art P., was a male, in his mid-30s. whose family had emigrated from Israel to the United States (Florida) when he was quite young. He was a well-respected health-care specialist in the San Francisco Bay Area, married 11 years (wife Sandra), with four children, three girls and a boy. He said his religion was still Judaism, and that he went to temple about once a month because "I like to feel there is someone looking after me other than myself."

He was seen individually for 14 sessions over a 6-month period. His presenting concern was that there was too much stress in his life, and he wanted to decrease and manage it better. On the SSCI he noted he wanted to develop more self-control "in relationships—with my wife and kids, my partners, and with myself; to be more calm, less abusive, less pushing people; to be a more upbeat person." He stated that he was embarrassed at how angry he often got: "I don't want my kids to see me yell and scream." He described himself as an overachiever, a perfectionist who didn't allow there to be loose ends; someone who had a low tolerance level, and pushed himself excessively. He showed many of the behavioral signs of the "Type A" personality, including forced, rapid speech, interrupting, visible facial tension, and somewhat aggressive "requests" about what the therapist could do for him to get rid of the stress "quickly" (Rosenman, 1978). Baseline self-observation of his weekly schedule revealed high job involvement—7 days a week, and 70 to 82 hours a week. In addition, his speciality required that he frequently be on call in the evening and weekends, and, when he was beeped on his pager, he often had to make quick decisions about potentially life-threatening issues.

Visual inspection of Figure Two preveals that his pretest scores on the four-quadrant control inventory indicate a quite high (2.84) quadrant three (negative assertive), and a quite low (1.93) quadrant two (positive yielding).

Initial baseline observation of stressors (antecedents), feelings of stress and being out of control (physiologically and cognitively), and consequences of "stress" took place during the first 2 weeks. Antecedent stressors ranged from daily hassles (losing his pen; workmen in his house during his afternoon off; wife forgetting to call plumbers to fix a leak; forced to wait on the phone 7 minutes for staff member to answer) to quite strong anxious feelings every time his "beeper" went off: "It's like my beeper is a cue to become tense."

He knew that he was feeling tense and out of control because his eyes would begin to focus double and he would look simultaneously at multiple things that he was trying to do; his mind would begin racing; his arms would feel heavy, his face and his chest sweaty; his stomach churning; and his heart beating rapidly. Often he would visibly shake, and his emotions ran the gamut from fear to raging anger. Once he reached that point, he would either become furious at those involved in the situation, or walk away—but in either case continue to perseverate on the stressor.

Based on information from the instrument, from the initial sessions, and from the self-observation material, a therapeutic intervention plan was formulated which consisted of three parts.

One part involved using the antecedent stressors (daily hassles and the beeper) as cues for relaxaton: deep, slow, abdominal breathing; cognitions that he wasn't going to let events "control" him and get the best of him—that he had the ability to head off a situation before it got out of hand.

The second part of the intervention involved teaching him a variety of assertive strategies (rather than quadrant-three aggressive strategies—blowing up, flying off the handle; or quadrant-four withdrawing strategies—walking away and ending up in a "dark hole funk," which were his normal style). This included learning to set boundaries and to state strongly and firmly his concerns, without "getting set off and blowing up."

The third aspect of the intervention involved teaching him self- (and other) acceptance. This included having him practice formal meditation, as well as daily cognitions. In the early sessions, there was considerable resistance to self-acceptance, because "I feel I can only be loved for what I do." He agreed he could say the following cognition: "I want to try and love and accept myself just as I am." After several weeks of practice, this evolved to "I can love and accept myself just as I am," and finally, he felt increasingly able to say—and believe—"I love and accept myself just as I am."

As can be seen from the post test scores in Figure Two and Table Two, his scores increased, as expected, for quadrant one (positive assertive). His score also increased (quite dramatically) for quadrant two (positive yielding). There was a slight decrease in quadrant three, negative assertive, in the expected direction. Quadrant four, negative yielding, increased slightly, an unexpected result.

His overall satisfaction scores (determined by the amount of "stay the same" across all four quadrants) decreased from 37.5%

TABLE TWO. Case One

	QUADRANT ONE			QUADRANT TWO		
	Pre	Post	F/U	Pre	Post	F/U
Sum of words	39	47	42	27	42	29
Number of words	16	16	16	14	14	14
Average ($\bar{x}$)	2.44	2.94	2.62	1.93	3.0	2.07
% Same	50% (8/16)	44% (7/16)	56% (9/16)	21% (3/14)	21% (3/14)	7% (1/14)
% More	50% (8/16)	50% (8/16)	44% (7/16)	64% (9/14)	79% (11/14)	93% (13/14)
% Less	--	6% (1/16)	--	14% (2/14)	--	--

OVERALL SATISFACTION (Percent wanting to stay the same across all four quadrants)	PRE
	37.5%
	(18/48)

on pretest to 32.6% on posttest. Table Two shows that, in terms of individual quadrants, even though his scores changed, his satisfaction level with quadrants one and four remained the same, and they decreased with quadrants two and three.

Inspecting individual words which are endorsed in the "unexpected" direction also is instructive. (The "unexpected" direction means to want "less" of a quadrant-one or quadrant-two word; or to want "more" of a quadrant-three or quadrant-four word.) For quadrant one on the pretest, Art stated that "purposeful" was something he wanted to be "more," whereas on the posttest it was something he wanted to be "less."

For quadrant two, he wanted to be "less" yielding and sensitive on the pretest, but on the post-test he wanted to be "more" yielding and sensitive. And for quadrant three, he said "aggressive" described him "very well" and he wanted to stay the "same" on the pretest, whereas on the post-test it still described him "very well" but he wanted to be "less" that way.

	QUADRANT THREE			QUADRANT FOUR	
Pre	Post	F/U	Pre	Post	F/U
37	37	35	8	9	9
13	14	13	5	5	5
2.84	2.64	2.69	1.6	1.8	1.8
31% (4/13)	21% (3/14)	15% (2/13)	60% (3/5)	60% (3/5)	40% (2/5)
--	--	--	--	--	--
69% (9/13)	79% (11/14)	85% (11/13)	40% (2/5)	40% (2/5)	60% (3/5)

POST	FOLLOW-UP
32.6% (16/49)	30.6% (15/49)

Case Two: Joyce M.

The client was a woman, in her mid-50s, who had been married for 35 years. She was white, born in the United States, and had no religious orientation: "I've tried, but I don't feel anything." She had a B.A., was a Phi Beta Kappa graduate, and had worked professionally one year (as a lab technician). She was a full-time housewife with "no children and no family" other than her husband.

She was seen for 19 sessions over a 9-month period. Her presenting complaint was "I want to learn how to better handle stress." She said she was feeling more and more anxious and stressed in her life; unable to cope; finding herself obsessing on details and unable to focus; and unable to make decisions about the smallest, most trivial questions (i.e., what size of microwave to buy) — "the smallest details overwhelm me." On the SSCI she noted two different attitudes toward self-control. On the one hand, she wanted to have

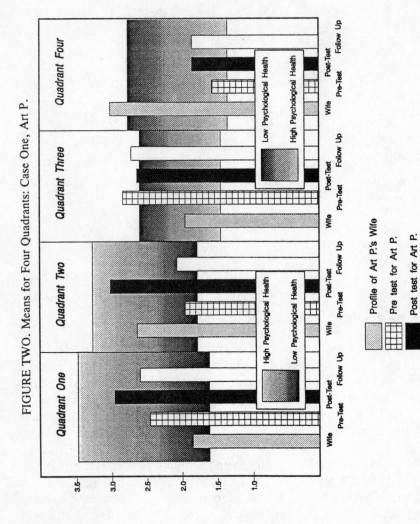

FIGURE TWO. Means for Four Quadrants: Case One, Art P.

less self-control—"I'm always trying to organize and collect things. I wish I weren't so obsessive and could just let go more." On the other hand, she wanted more self-control—in the areas of stress and overeating. She described herself as a perfectionist, on the nervous side, moving too fast, never being able to react well to immediate decisions.

About a year and half previously, her husband had had a serious illness (from which he subsequently recovered). At that time she had gone into psychoanalytically oriented therapy. Her husband's illness had made her realize how lonely, and socially isolated, she was, which saddened and depressed her. She was searching for values, a sense of meaning in a broader sense—"an anchor, something to hold onto. I've let my life slip through my fingers—no parents, no profession, no family." On the Beck depression scale, she scored 17, indicating a mild to moderate depression (Beck & Beanesderfer, 1974). She was on two medications: mellaril and librium—"I don't think they do any good, but I'm afraid to stop taking them."

Visual inspection of Figure Three reveals a pretest profile on the four-quadrant instrument nearly exactly the opposite of high psychological health (i.e., low psychological health. Quadrant four, negative yielding, was the highest, followed by quadrant three, negative assertive. Both the negative quadrants were higher than the positive quadrants, with quadrant one, positive assertive (1.53) being the lowest of all.

The initial weeks of therapy involved self-observation of stress (how she knew when she was stressed; how strong the stress was; what caused the stress; and how she reacted to the stress). She did a conscientious job of the self-observation (with the exception of the issue of intensity. She said she wasn't able to make a decision about "how strong" the stress was—that made her more stressed trying to decide—so she didn't monitor that part).

She described feelings of stress as "little butterflies" in her stomach; thoughts running dramatically; tightness in her chest; and an overall shakiness and jitteriness in her body. (During the initial sessions, she often pulled at the skin on her neck and/or picked at her eyebrows). After the initial self-observation phase, Joyce wondered whether it had been worthwhile to learn so much about her stress, because she didn't feel as though she were getting any better, but rather even becoming more stressed.

Events that made her nervous ranged from waking up in the morning and not being able to focus her thoughts (she was seen at the memory clinic, and organic dysfunction was ruled out); worrying whether she would be able to cook a good meal for her gourmet class; a phone call from a person in the class asking if another guest could come — "that made me very stressed because I wasn't able to control who was coming to my party." In a similar vein related to control, she said that unexpected inputs were hard for her; and, when she did try to act assertively, she felt quite guilty afterwards. To calm herself when she felt stressed, she would watch TV a bit (did help — particularly the soaps); drink a glass of wine (didn't help); go have her hair done (did help). Her more usual ways of reacting, she noted, were to "leave the situation — become lethargic, sleep; disinterested in doing anything"; or cut out recipes compulsively; go 10 directions at once, accomplishing nothing; eat a lot; nibble at food.

Based on information from the self-observation, the SSCI, and the four-quadrant instrument, a four part intervention was undertaken.

The first part of the intervention dealt with stress management. Joyce was given a relaxation/meditation tape (Shapiro, 1977) and instructed to practice formally once a day; and contingent meditation (self-modeling and self-instructions) as needed and as cued by anxiety. Further, since it seemed that some anxiety was functional for her (motivated her to act), she was told to pay particular attention to focusing herself — learning to concentrate and pay attention in a soft, careful manner.

Overall, during the course of therapy, she said the tapes were of marginal help. She said she would feel relaxed (sometimes) while listening to the tape ("I don't have my usual hurry-up feeling while playing it") but there was little carry over effect. Also, at times listening to the tape made her breathing seem unnatural, and she felt her pulse accelerating. Further, she sometimes became angry with the tapes, and argumentative. When the tape would say "There's nothing for you to do now but relax, there is no pressure. . . . " she would think to herself, "I have lots of places to go and lots to do."

Later in therapy, Joyce was given Stroebel's (1983) "quieting reflex training." She said the best part of it was the material about fight or flight, which helped her to realize how she overreacts to situations. However, she didn't like that tape either—she began crying while trying it because she couldn't remember what order to do the relaxation in; she was impatient because there was so much silence; and also the tape made her see how negative she was: "When the tape said you're feeling beautiful, I felt 'yucchy'; I didn't feel limp and heavy, and I certainly didn't feel like sunshine."

She had a great deal of difficulty with visualization. The most effective parts of stress training for her were focusing exercises and self-instructions.

A second part of the intervention involved social skills/assertiveness training. She noted that when she got angry she became emotional and unable to speak. We worked on her being able to use anger and upsetness as a cue to relax; and then to calmly state her preferences. The first time this worked (with her husband), she felt a tremendous sense of competence.

Social skills, to increase her contacts with others and remove her from her isolated daily life, were a mixed blessing. On the one hand, she did get involved in more activities, volunteer groups, playing golf, visiting friends, and so was less isolated. However, she felt that going out and seeing others only showed her how competent everyone else was, and how miserable and alone she was.

A third area of intervention dealt with exercise and weight control. She did develop a program of exercise, including both golf and swimming, and also of monitoring and "gradually" reducing the high-caloric binge eating.

The final area had to do with cognitions related to her self-concept and sense of competence. We worked on a cognitive therapy reframing "I make myself upset when I demand that . . . I be better than or equal to others; have as much staying power as younger women; not forgetting things," and the follow up line: "I can love myself even when . . . I forget things, etc." (Piaget & Binkley, 1982).

In addition, Joyce completed a reinforcement survey schedule, and then, on a weekly basis, monitored mastery and pleasure experiences.

Within the sessions, an intervention consisted of taking the first few minutes to relate only positive experiences from the previous week. Initially this was difficult for her, and each positive ended in a "but": "I won at a bridge contest but the woman across from me blew smoke in my face and I hated it." However, soon she could do it quite well, and even joked about it. "This week something good happened, and I got so excited . . . . I said to myself thank God I would have something positive to tell you . . . and then I thought to myself, I just know I'll forget this before I see him!" Besides smiling and even some laughter in the later sessions, she also began to wear brighter clothes and some makeup.

As can be seen from Figure Three and Table Three, with the exception of quadrant two (positive yielding) which stayed the same, all of the other three quadrants moved in the expected direction, with the largest movement being a decrease in negative yielding (quadrant four) from 3.4 to 2.8.

Her overall self-satisfaction score increased from 23% on pretest to 40% on post-test. She was more satisfied with herself in quadrants two, three, and four; but less satisfied with herself in quadrant one (positive assertiveness).

In terms of words endorsed in the non-expected direction, on the pretest for quadrant two, she wanted to be "less" yielding, accepting, and letting go; whereas on the posttest she wanted to be "more" letting go; and, since her self-perception had changed from very to moderately, she now wanted to be the "same" in accepting and yielding. On quadrant three, on the pretest, she wanted to be "more" rigid, aggressive, and dogmatic; on the posttest she wanted to be the "same" dogmatic; but "less" rigid (her self-perception of "rigid" had changed from not at all on pretest to very rigid on post test). She still wanted to be "more" aggressive.

Follow-Up for Cases One and Two

Seven months after individual therapy ended with client one, and 10 months after therapy ended with client two, a follow-up four quadrant assessment was completed. (It should be noted that 3 months after the end of individual therapy, case one requested and received two "booster" sessions on stress management.)

As can be seen from Figures Two and Three, there was slippage in the therapeutic progress for both clients, more dramatic for case two than case one.

For case one, the follow-up data shows change in the undesirable direction in three of the quadrants (and no change in quadrant four). However, quadrants one, two, and three are still indicative of more psychological health than at pretest. The overall satisfaction score was 30.6%, a continued drop from post-test. Quadrants one, two, and three satisfaction scores (7%,15%, and 40% respectively) were lower than at either pre- or post-test. Quadrant one, positive assertive, satisfaction score (56%) was higher than either pre- or post-test.

The results of follow-up for case two can be seen in Figure Three. In every quadrant except quadrant two (where there was no change), the profile is indicative of less psychological health than at pretest. Her overall satisfaction score was 30.6%, higher than pretest, but a drop from post-test. Satisfaction scores for quadrants two and three (50% and 36% respectively) dropped from post-test, but were higher than pretest. Quadrant one satisfaction (19%) was lower than pre or post-test; and quadrant four satisfaction returned to 0%.

DISCUSSION

It is clear from the post-test data administered at the end of the individual therapy sessions that psychotherapy did help both individuals increase their overall "psychological health" as measured by a four-quadrant model of control. This is true even though the initial profiles of the two individuals were quite different. It is also clear, based on the follow-up data, that there was relapse and slippage in therapeutic gains for both patients, and that a truly comprehensive control-based model of psychotherapy will have to specifically tackle this issue of maintenance of clinical improvement after therapy has been completed.

TABLE THREE. Case Two

	QUADRANT ONE			QUADRANT TWO		
	Pre	Post	F/U	Pre	Post	F/U
Sum of Words	23	25	22	28	28	28
Number of Words	15	15	16	14	14	14
Average ($\bar{x}$)	1.53	1.66	1.37	2.0	2.0	2.0
% Same	33.3% 5/15	20% 3/15	18.7% 3/16	21% 3/14	64.3% 9/14	50% 7/14
%More	66.6% 10/15	80% 12/15	81.3% 13/16	57% 8/14	35.7% 5/14	35.7% 5/14
% Less	--	--	--	21% 3/14	--	14.3% 2/14

OVERALL SATISFACTION (Percent of wanting to stay the same across all four quadrants)	PRE 23.4% 11/47

Clinical Applications of the Four-Quadrant Inventory

There are several clinical benefits to be obtained from the use of the four-quadrant control instrument. It can provide confirmatory information for the therapist's clinical impressions about a client's "control identity" and issues. In particular, it provides an understanding of the client's self-perception along four control dimensions; offers an index of client's "self-satisfaction" with his or her current identity, and indicates areas where improvement is desired; and it can "red flag" specific areas where clients endorse words in an "unexpected direction."

In addition to helping gather that information, the inventory can provide a model for a vision of psychological health from a control perspective. It may be argued that this beginning model of positive

QUADRANT THREE			QUADRANT FOUR		
Pre	Post	F/U	Pre	Post	F/U
30	29	35	17	14	18
13	13	14	5	5	5
2.31	2.23	2.5	3.4	2.8	3.6
23%	38%	35.7%	0%	40%	0%
3/13	5/13	5/14	0/5	2/5	0/5
23%	8%	7%	--	--	--
3/13	1/13	1/14			
54%	54%	57.1%	100%	60%	100%
7/13	7/13	8/14	5/5	3/5	5/5

	POST		FOLLOW-UP		
	40.4%		30.6%		
	19/47		15/49		

psychological health is quite important as a way to counter the historical emphasis on pathology-based models of human nature (Walsh & Shapiro, 1983). Without some kind of model of positive psychological health to guide self-control strategies, Nolan (1974) has noted that the techniques themselves, or unexamined cultural mores may determine the goals of therapy.

The four-quadrant model may help not only in the formulation of the vision of psychological health for clinicians, but also as a teaching tool to use with clients. The four quadrants can help clients differentiate two positive styles of dealing with the world: an active control, and a letting-go control. This may broaden their understanding (and eventually their behavioral repertoire) of coping strategies. Further, an important part of a control based model of psychotherapy is helping clients differentiate and clarify which aspects of their concerns are under their potential control, and which are not. The model of the four quadrants (as well as feedback on their

FIGURE THREE. Means for Four Quadrants: Case Two, Joyce M.

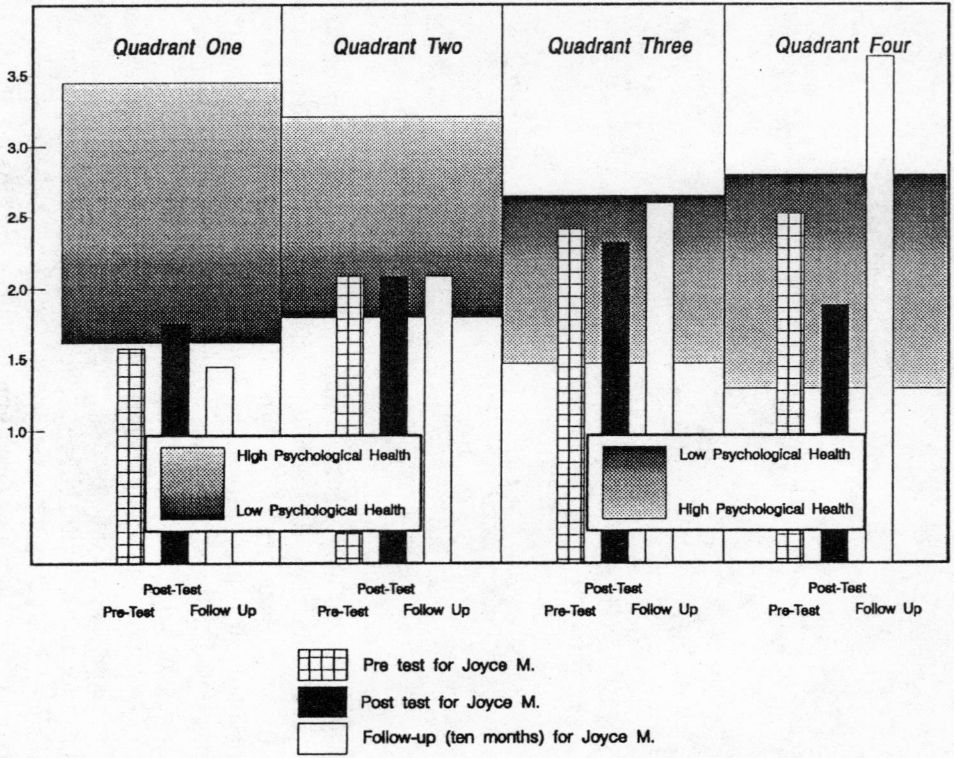

own views of themselves) can provide important information to the client, and help in the understanding and selection of appropriate strategies. It can be a teaching tool to suggest to clients that perhaps it is not (as in case one) that he wants to be less sensitive and less yielding (quadrant-two words) but rather less timid and passive (quadrant-four words). The model can also show that it doesn't need to be an either/or situation between positive, active modes of control and positive, yielding modes of control, but that individuals can learn a combination (and integration) of both quadrants one and two.

This combination and balance is clearly illustrated in the two cases described in this article. Case one may be described as having aspects of a "Type A" behavior pattern—a person who had too much need to control the world in an active, assertive manner—which often led him to feeling aggressive (quadrant three) or in a dark hole funk (quadrant four). Case two was an example of a person with aspects of a "learned helplessness" (Seligman, 1975) anxiety/depression who felt there was very little she could competently or effectively do. Although both were suffering considerable stress, the causes of the stress were quite different for each; and their self-perceived "control identity" on the four-quadrant instrument was quite different. Thus, the goal of therapy for each, and the interventions selected were accordingly weighted and balanced differently. In case one, there was some emphasis on learning to shift aggression into appropriate assertiveness; however, most of the emphasis was on how to relax, let go control, and accept and enjoy more of the process of life. In case two, there was some emphasis on self-acceptance and relaxation, but more emphasis on active, assertive strategies to give her a sense of competence with the outside world.

The use of the two positive control strategies—assertive and yielding—are not either/or propositions, but a question of balance. And the pretest profile based on the four-quadrant inventory can help give both therapist and client information about where there is imbalance that needs to be addressed. Further, posttest assessment, using the four quadrant inventory, can see how effective the interventions have been in dealing with that imbalance.

Caveats and Future Research
with the Four-Quadrant
Inventory

The results of this article, a preliminary investigation detailing two cases, must be interpreted with caution for several reasons. First, there are clear (and intentional) demand characteristics present. In both cases, the four-quadrant model was presented to the clients by the therapist, and the goals of therapy were explicitly spelled out. There could have been a desire by the clients to please the therapist on the posttest.

Second, although the pre/post changes were almost all in the expected direction (except for quadrant four in case one; and the no change of quadrant two in case two), the changes were for the most part small. Further, in case two, the profile was one of low psychological health to begin with (with quadrants three and four higher than one and two; and, though improved by post-test, quadrants three and four were still larger than one and two).

Third, additional research needs to demonstrate concurrent validity of the four quadrant inventory to ensure that self-perception measured by a paper and pencil test has observable cognitive and/or behavioral task correlates.

Although this instrument and the data so far collected provide a good beginning at defining positive psychological health, future research, with larger Ns, is needed to more precisely define the gradients of the continuum between low and high psychological health. Also, profiles of clinical populations with "control problems" need to be developed. This could include profiles of those with addictive disorders (anorexia, bulimia, obesity, smoking, alcohol, and drugs), "Type A" individuals, compulsive gamblers, "violence-prone individuals," and those with learned-helplessness "depressions." These profiles should help provide us with a more precise assessment and measuring tool, and hopefully, one day, with some ability at predictive validity.

Within the instrument itself, additional research is necessary to ensure that the quadrants can be relatively "independent" of each other, that is, quadrant one can increase and quadrant two stay the same. A simple validations study with three groups: (1) assertiveness training; (2) relaxation training; and (3) a non-intervention (control) group could help determine that.

Further research will need to continue to refine and to make more precise the relationship of the four quadrants to each other, as well as to refine and make more precise the variables within each quadrant itself. For example, regarding quadrant three, case two said the words "impatient, tense, rigid" described her very well, but "manipulative, overcontrolling, and pushy" described her "not well at all." Are there two different dimensions within quadrant three? Regarding quadrant two, do words like "calm," "accepting" reflect a different dimension than words like "nurturing"? And, in quadrant one, case two described herself as high on "logical, rational, and responsible," but low on the other dimensions. Could there be two different dimensions within quadrant one that further factor analysis needs to refine? And finally, the word "past oriented" in quadrant four needs reconsideration.

Another aspect of the four-quadrant instrument that needs further investigation is the "overall satisfaction with self score: i.e., how much a person wants to stay the same. Case two increased in satisfaction with herself over the course of therapy. This was expected, and could be interpreted as a sign of increased self-acceptance, and ego real/ego ideal integration. However, case one, which I would subjectively state was the "more successful" of the two cases, decreased in overall satisfaction with self from pre- to post-test, contrary to what I would have anticipated. Post hoc, I might rationalize that it was a sign he became less defensive by the end of therapy! More data, and more thought on how to interpret this score is clearly warranted.

A final question raised by the inventory is how to interpret an individual's selection of a word in the "non-expected" direction. For example, case two said she wanted to be less accepting and more aggressive. It seems this may be a sign of extreme frustration at the situation and quite low self-acceptance. However, again, further research is necessary.

There was one provocative finding about couples from this study, which was serendipitous, and which suggests an interesting area of future research using the four-quadrant instrument to develop profiles of couples (and then looking at how those profiles correlate with the "success" of the relationship). For example, in case one, there was an opportunity to meet the spouse during one of the middle sessions. She took the four-quadrant instrument, and her profile was almost a stereotyped sex-role reversal of her husband's. As can be seen from Figure Two, his quadrants one and three were, respectively, higher than his quadrants two and four; whereas her quadrants two and four, respectively, were higher than her quadrants three and one. Their profiles were almost an inverse of each other. Is this the initial attraction of opposites? Did they grow, in the years of their marriage, in this complementary or inverse fashion? Is it that their styles are now too far apart, so that what once attracted became grating?

The Shapiro Self-Control Inventory (SSCI)

Data from the SSCI provided additional interesting information in three areas: (1) motivation; (2) belief in ability to change; and (3) willingness to be taught — germane to developing a control-based model of psychotherapy. Topics on the Inventory related to motivation included: (1.1) reasons you want to change — positive benefits and advantages from changing; (1.2) what are the consequences if no change is made; (1.3) what are "excuses" you might give to sabotage your own efforts to change; and (1.4) what might be the negative consequences if you do succeed in changing. There were then three questions (using a four-point Likert scale from very much to not at all) asking: After reviewing the above responses, (a) how strongly do you feel you want to make change in the areas; (b) how willing do you feel you are to learn and regularly practice change strategies; and (c) do you consider yourself to be a highly motivated person? The topic of motivation is a crucial one to explore with the client prior to the actual teaching of the self-control strategies in order to reduce the risk of self-sabotage, and to provide a clear understanding about the reasons for the efforts toward change. Such information can be referred to in order to help encourage the client in continuing to adhere to the self-control strategies during difficult times.

Case one was quite strongly motivated to change: "I'm unwilling to continue to live with the amount of stress I've had these past years," and "I know I'll have a heart attack or quit my work unless I can overcome this stress." He also felt successful change would make him happier and a "better human being." Regarding potential difficult times ahead if he does try to change, he said finding the time to get to counseling sessions, as well as the time to practice the self-control strategies; but regarding sabotaging his own efforts, he said, "I won't." In terms of potentially negative consequences if he succeeded, he felt he might not continue to be as wealthy or as prominent as he currently was. On a four-point scale, he very much wanted to make changes, was very willing to learn and regularly practice change strategies, and was very highly motivated.

Case two was much less committed to change. She felt that although there were positive consequences for change—feel better about myself, it probably affects my asthma—the consequences of not changing were "none in particular"; "I guess I would continue to be dissatisfied with myself and my husband would be annoyed." Regarding stumbling blocks to change, she listed "too busy," "I'll forget"; and in terms of self-sabotage, she said she might say the techniques were a "waste of time—watching a soap opera may be better." She did say she couldn't think of any negative consequences of succeeding—except maybe she would be so relaxed she would just lie around all day—"but I can't really imagine that." On the Likert-type scale for motivation, she was "somewhat" strongly motivated to change, was very willing to practice change strategies, and considered herself to be a person with a "low level of motivation."

The second area on the SSCI had to do with beliefs about one's ability to change. Questions reflecting this asked: (2.1) In the past, when you have tried to change, how successful have you been? (2.2) How much self-control do you believe you have? (2.3) In general, do you believe if you really try something, you can accomplish it? (2.4/2.5) Do you believe you have the ability to control your thoughts? your feelings? (2.6) Do you believe that there are skills that can be learned which could enable you to increase your self-control?

Case one said he "strongly believed" he could accomplish what he tried. "I always succeed," he stated, and then proceeded to describe his past history of losing 80 pounds and of stopping smoking. "This behavioral stuff is great!" However, he "somewhat disbelieved he could control his thoughts and feelings."

Case two said she had always wanted to be in control of situations, but had never exhibited positive high self-control in the past. She "somewhat believed" if she realy tried something she could accomplish it, "but I don't really have much confidence." She "somewhat disbelieved" she could control her thoughts, "not when they are shooting all over the place." Regarding her feelings, she endorsed the "somewhat disbelieve" category also, and noted she didn't show emotions too much: "I don't like to lose control of my feelings — like anger, or crying." Regarding her belief that skills existed which could be learned and which could enable her to increase her self-control she responded, "I hope there are; I don't understand; I have to believe there are; I think maybe not."

A third relevant area from the SSCI deals with how willing a person is to be taught (called the "freedom reflex" after Pavlov's dog experiments). This is an important topic for the therapist to address in order to know the most effective ways to teach the techniques, and to have some idea of the level of resistance that may be encountered. Case one said he was strongly willing to be taught: "I'm the susceptible type." Case two said she was "somewhat willing" to be taught, and noted she had to be "browbeaten into change."

Future Directions for a Control-Based
Model of Psychotherapy

There are several important areas which further research should pursue to help more closely connect the broad, metalevel aspects of a control theory to the practical, detailed clinical applications of a control-based model of psychotherapy. This includes efforts at bringing several different literatures, from animal models of control, to social psychological studies of perceived control, to the literature on both Eastern and Western self-control strategies.

For example, future research could undertake a content analysis of the verbal behavior of the therapy sessions (Gottschalk & Glesser, 1969; Gottschalk et al., 1986) along previously identified dimensions of the self-control—choice, responsibility, motivation, skill, goal, and awareness (Shapiro, 1983a). This could help determine changes across particular dimensions over the course of therapy. Further, these changes could be refined by seeing what domains (i.e., professional, interpersonal relations, spiritual, body, mind) control problems occurred in over the course of therapy (Shapiro & Shapiro, 1983, 1984), as well as during developmental stages of an individual's life (i.e., Levinson, 1978).

The "dynamics" of control also need to be addressed. For example, a self-control history seems increasingly important to understand parental views of control and discipline, as well as the client's own history of control efforts. Issues of "self" and identity also need to be better incorporated within the model. For example, is there a way to concretize negative self-image with respect to control? Are there certain individuals who have a greater "need for control" than others? In addition, more attention needs to be focused on patient/therapist control issues, including what are the best ways to deal with resistance and to teach the self-control strategies.

Additional concerted efforts at refinement and precision on these issues, as well as on the four-quadrant instrument and the SSCI should help clinicians and therapists be better able to pinpoint the type of stress, its cause, and the control-related issues involved. This, in turn, should help us more effectively select (and teach) the appropriate self-control intervention(s).

NOTES

1. The concept of self-control as accepting, yielding, and "letting go control" is sometimes difficult for Western educated individuals to understand. Although this notion is found in the Eastern psychological literature (cf., Shapiro, 1978), it may be helpful to clarify it with reference to the work on the components of self-control (Shapiro, 1983a). "Letting go control," accepting, and yielding can be an example of self-control if they meet the six criteria described in that article. Specifically, letting go control may be (1) a goal which is (2) chosen with (3) awareness, and for which one assumes (4) responsibility. It may require (5) discipline to achieve that goal, as well as certain cognitive (6) skills.

2. In the first analysis of this data on psychological health, a comparison was made between six different prompts: high and low psychological health for man, woman, person. There were some significant differences, generally in an atypically sex-role stereotyped direction (e.g., words associated with quadrant one

were seen as significantly more a sign of high psychological health for a woman than for a man, etc.) (Shapiro, 1983d). However, after subsequent rater-reliability studies (Shapiro, 1982a), additional data analyses were performed. One of the computations involved a cluster analysis (Shapiro, 1985), which revealed that the high psychological health prompts for person, man, woman clustered together; and the low prompts for person, man, woman clustered together. Therefore, for simplicity sake, the data for high psychological health were grouped to develop one profile; as were the data for low psychological health.

    3. Shapiro, D.H. The Shapiro Self-Control Inventory. (SSCI) (3rd revision). Unpublished inventory. University of California, Irvine.

REFERENCES

Brownell, K.D., Marlatt, G.A., Lichtenstein, E., & Wilson, G.T. (1986). Understanding and preventing relapse. *American Psychologist, 41*(7),765-782.

Beck, A., & Beanesderfer. A. (1974). Assessment of depression: The depression inventory. In P. Pichot (Ed.), *Psychological measurements and psychopharmacology: Modern problems in pharmacopsychiatry* (Vol. 7, pp. 151-169). Basil, Switzerland: Karger.

Eliot, R.S., & Breo, D.L. (1984). *Is it worth dying for?* New York: Bantam Books.

Friedman, M., & Ulmer, D. (1984). *Treating Type A behavior and your heart.* New York: Ballantine.

Gottschalk, L.A. (1986). Research using the Gottschalk-Gleser content analysis scales in English since 1969. In G. Gottschalk, F. Lolas, and L. Viney, (Eds.), *Content analysis of verbal behavior.* New York: Springer-Verlag.

Gottschalk, L.A., & Gleser, G. (1969). *The measurement of psychological states through the content analysis of verbal behavior.* Berkeley: University of California Press.

Jacob, R.G., & Chesney, M.A. (1984). Stress management for cardiovascular reactivity. *Annals of Behavioral Medicine, 6*(4), 23-27.

Jeffery, R.W. (1987). Behavioral treatment of obesity. *Annals of Behavioral Medicine, 9*(1), 20-24.

Levinson, D. (1978). *Seasons of a man's life.* New York: Knopf.

Nathan, P. (1986). Outcomes of treatment for alcoholism: Current data. *Annals of Behavioral Medicine, 8*(2-3), 40-45.

Nolan, J.D. (1972). Freedom and dignity: A functional analysis. *American Psychologist, 29,* 157-160.

Pelletier, K. (1977). *Mind as healer, mind as slayer.* New York: Delacorte.

Piaget, G., & Binkley, B. (1982). *Barriers!* New York: Irvington Press.

Rodin, J. (1986). Aging and health: Effects of the sense of control. *Science, 233,* 1271-1276.

Rosenman, R. (1978). The interview method of assessment of the coronary-prone behavior pattern. In T.M. Dembroski, S. Weiss, and M Reinleig (Eds.), *Coronary-prone behavior* (pp. 55-69). New York: Springer.

Selye H. (1974). *Stress without distress*. Philadelphia: Lippincott.

Seligman, M.E.P. (1975). *Helplessness*. San Francisco: Freeman.

Shapiro, D.H. (1977). Clinical instructions in meditation and behavioral self-control. In C. Franks (Ed.), *Behavior Therapy Tape Series*. New York: BMA/Guillford.

Shapiro, D.H. (1978). *Precision Nirvana*. Englewood Cliffs, NJ: Prentice-Hall.

Shapiro, D.H. (1978a). Instructions for a training package combining Zen meditation and behavioral self management strategies. *Psychologia, 21*, 70-76.

Shapiro, D.H. (1980). *Meditation: Self regulation strategy and altered state of consciousness*, New York: Aldine.

Shapiro, D.H. (1982). Comparison of meditation with other self-control strategies: Biofeedback, hypnosis, progressive relaxation: A review of the clinical and physiological literature. *American Journal of Psychiatry, 139*(3), 267-274.

Shapiro, D.H. (1982a). Reliability of four quadrant model of self-control: Ratings by experts in Type A Behavior/Health Psychology; East-West Psychology, and sex role psychology. *Psychologia: An International Journal of Psychology in the Orient, 25*(3), 149-154.

Shapiro, D.H. (1983a). A content analysis of views of self-control. *Biofeedback and self-regulation, 8*(1),73-86.

Shapiro, D.H. (1983b). Dimensions relevant to the health care and therapeutic use of self-control strategies: A systems model for applied research. *Perspectives in Biology and Medicine, 26*(4), 91-116.

Shapiro, D.H. (1983c). Self-Control and positive health. In R. Walsh and D. H. Shapiro (Eds.), *Beyond health and normality: Toward a vision of exceptional psychological health* (pp. 371-387). New York: Van Nostrand Reinhold.

Shapiro, D.H. (1983d). Self-control: Refinement of a construct. *Biofeedback and Self-Regulation, 8*(3) 443-460.

Shapiro, D.H. (1983e). A factor analytic study of perceived characteristics of person, man, and woman with high and low psychological health: Relation to a model of control. *Psychologia: An International Journal of Psychology in the Orient, 26*(3) 142-158.

Shapiro, D.H. (1989a). Self-control and other-control in cross cultural perspective: Balinese trance and religious beliefs. *ReVision: The Journal of Consciousness and Change, 12*(2), 33-46.

Shapiro, D.H., & Bates, D.E. (1989). The measurement of control and self-control: Background, rationale, description of a control content analysis scale. Manuscript submitted for publication.

Shapiro, D.H., Evans, G., & Shapiro, J. (1987). Human control. *Science, 238*, 260.

Shapiro, D.H., & Shapiro, J. (1980). The clinical management of stress: Non-pharmacological approaches. *Family Practice Recertification, 2*(10), 55-63.

Shapiro, D.H., & Shapiro, J. (1983). Self-control concerns for men and women:

Refinement and extension of a contsruct. *Journal of Clinical Psychology*, *39*(6), 878-892.

Shapiro, D.H., & Zifferblatt, S. (1976). Zen meditation and behavioral self con-trol: Similarities, differences, clinical applications. *American Psychologist*, *31*, 519-532.

Shapiro, J., & Shapiro, D.H. (1984). Self-control and relationship: Toward a model of interpersonal health. *Journal of Humanistic Psychology*, *24*(4), 91-116.

Shapiro, J., & Shapiro, D. (1979). The psychology of responsibility. *New England Journal of Medicine*, *301*, 211-212.

Stroebel, C.F. (1983). *Quieting reflex for adults*. New York: BMA/Guillford.

Walsh, R.N., & Shapiro, D.H. (Eds.). (1983). *Beyond health and normality: Explorations of exceptional psychological wellbeing*. New York: Van Nostrand Reinhold.